The Last Foundling

TOM H. MACKENZIE was born in London in 1939 to an unmarried mother who gave him up to the Foundling Hospital. He was one of the last children to be taken in by the institution, which had been providing care for unfortunate infants for over two hundred years. Following a spell in the army, Tom became active in business and opened several health clubs, a ski centre and a locksmith and cobbler shop. Tom has three grown-up children and lives in Plymouth with his wife Ausra. He writes a regular column for the *Plymouth Herald*.

The Last Foundling

TOM H. MACKENZIE

PAN BOOKS

First published 2014 by Pan Books
an imprint of Pan Macmillan
20 New Wharf Road, London N1 9RR
Associated companies throughout the world
www.panmacmillan.com

ISBN 978-1-4472-5326-6

5 7 9 8 6

A CIP catalogue record for this book is available from the British Library.

Typeset by Palimpsest Book Production Limited, Falkirk, Stirlingshire
Printed and bound by CPI Group (UK) Ltd, Croydon, CR0 4YY

Visit **www.panmacmillan.com** to read more about all our books
and to buy them. You will also find features, author interviews and
news of any author events, and you can sign up for e-newsletters
so that you're always first to hear about our new releases.

To my Mother

Contents

PROLOGUE
Tom H. Mackenzie, 2013

IT IS A BRIGHT BUT CHILLY MORNING as I sit outside a little cafe in Berkhamsted enjoying my first coffee of the day. I pull my coat tightly around my chest and feel a deep sense of calm. I am content. My health is good, and except for the odd twinge in my back, I count myself fortunate to be weathering my seventy-four years so well. I have a loving wife and three grown-up children of whom I am immensely proud. And after years of slaving away at various business ventures, I have found a quieter pace of life as a cobbler and locksmith in Plympton, a busy suburb of the city of Plymouth. There's nothing better than the smell of leather and polish in the morning, and with my wife by my side and a steady stream of customers always eager to stop and chat, life is never dull.

As the people of Berkhamsted walk past my table, negotiating the cobbles in new suede boots, soft leather gloves and quilted Barbour jackets, it strikes me how affluent this

1

most ancient of market towns has become. It is now, I am told, part of the stockbroker belt and a very popular place for those who work in London to bring up their children. A little boy races past, trying to catch up with his sister, and I feel a sudden wave of envy as I remember my own childhood here. Although I now belong in this scene – a cappuccino and the flaky remains of a croissant before me and my gas-guzzling car parked up the road – it was not always so.

When I was first brought here in 1944, I was on the lowest step of the many-runged ladder that was British society. I was four years old and about to start at a school for those who, like me, were illegitimate and had been given up by their mothers at birth. The stigma of illegitimacy was still so strong in those days that young mothers who were given no support by their child's father struggled to survive. There were no welfare provisions as there are today, and the censure a young woman faced – both from society and from close family – made bringing up a child outside marriage almost impossible.

When my mother found out that she was expecting a baby in 1938, she knew that she couldn't keep me, however much she wanted to. Her boyfriend was on the other side of the world trying to set up a new life for them both, and the thought of telling her conservative Presbyterian parents was too frightening to contemplate. Holding on to the hope that she might one day be in a position to reclaim me, she turned to the governors of the Foundling Hospital in London and asked them to accept her baby.

The Foundling Hospital was founded in the eighteenth century by a retired sea captain, Thomas Coram, who despaired to see so many poor infants abandoned and dying in the streets of the capital and spent years campaigning for something to be done to provide care and education for vulnerable children. In 1739, after two decades of petitioning, he finally succeeded in obtaining a royal charter, and children began to pass through the charity's doors in 1741.

In the early years, the charity was threatened by escalating costs which made closure a real possibility, and Parliament stepped in to help, but at a price: it would provide an annual subsidy on condition that the Hospital accepted all unwanted babies. Up until then the Hospital had only admitted a quota of infants. As part of the selection process they used ballots, in which women would put their hands into a bag and take out a ball. If the ball was white, they were in; if it was black, they were rejected; and if it was red, they were put on a reserve list – and all this was dependent on the outcome of a health check. The Hospital pursued a policy of admitting only those infants that it judged to have a strong chance of survival. Acutely aware that its resources were limited, and in an age of high infant mortality, it did not feel that it was wise to do otherwise.

3

TOM H. MACKENZIE

When it got to the point that the Hospital's dire finances made a bargain with Parliament necessary, the results were disastrous. A large number of the babies admitted died, but not before they had infected many of the healthy ones. Coram must have despaired to see his life's work, his family of happy infants, falling to the ravages of disease, and it could not be allowed to continue. He parted ways with Parliament and regained independence by prevailing upon the rich and powerful men of his day to lend their financial support. He reinstated health as a principle of selection and the Hospital later tightened the application process further, only accepting babies from women who they considered to have good morals but who had been abandoned or suffered genuine misfortune.

The most common reason for a mother to give up her baby was the same in the early twentieth century as it was in the early eighteenth – a child born out of wedlock brought shame on the mother, leading to ostracization and hardship. The mothers giving up their babies to the care of the Hospital were initially required to leave details about their birth, parentage and history so that if they were later in a position to reclaim them, they could do so. In practice such reconciliations were rare and, by my day, virtually unheard of. Indeed, extraordinary measures were taken to preserve the anonymity of the children so that at the age of fifteen, if they hadn't been reclaimed, they could leave the Hospital and start new lives without the stain of

4

illegitimacy. These meant new names and new clothes for those who were admitted, and no visits, or even letters, from their mothers.

I was born Derek Craig on 14 May 1939 but became Tom Humphreys nine weeks later. I've no doubt that the governors had good intentions, but in taking away our names, putting us in matching uniforms, and making us follow the same strict routine, they stripped us of our identities. The problem was that the Hospital's attitude towards children hadn't changed much since the eighteenth century. There was no attempt to understand our emotional needs or the importance of maintaining close relationships between parents and children. It wasn't even an issue.

Evidence of this outdated view was the Hospital's procedure, which was to foster out young infants until they were old enough to be disciplined and could join the main school, and then, at the age of four or five, to rip them from the only families they had ever known and thrust them into an institution where no one would give them a hug if they were upset or even a kiss goodnight. I, like so many foundlings, had grown up thinking of my foster parents as Mum and Dad and their house as home. The terrible sense of rejection and abandonment I experienced when I was sent to the Hospital was hard to overcome, and many of the children, myself included, suffered from anxiety. There was a lot of crying, nail-biting and bedwetting in those early years.

It's tragic to think that this second loss of a mother, which was undeniably more of a wrench than the first, could have been avoided. To make matters worse, the regime at the Foundling Hospital was severe and unvarying. We were subjected to harsh discipline, and every day was made up of the same routine of chores, lessons and church. Historically, foundlings would go on to accept lowly positions when it was time to leave – the boys in the military and the girls in service – and although more opportunities were becoming available in the twentieth century, the Hospital still prioritized obedience and biblical instruction over developing our minds to their full potential.

The original Foundling Hospital in Bloomsbury was an imposing building with two wings, finely wrought-iron gates and walls adorned with paintings by the greatest artists of the day, but having decided that London was too polluted a place to bring up children, the governors moved the school to a brand new, purpose-built building in Berkhamsted in 1935. It housed six hundred abandoned boys and girls and became my home for ten years. As a child I thought it was grand, if intimidating – a great sprawling pile that towered over the town and included a concert hall, dining room, indoor swimming pool, gymnasium, chapel and acres of beautifully manicured grounds. I was always proud that the steeple could be seen for miles around – it was a landmark that situated us in the community and served as a reminder that we were there and not to be forgotten. But having spent two hundred years in its London building, the charity was not to spend the next two hundred in this. Attitudes were finally changing, and with the Curtis Report in 1946, national policy moved towards adoption over institutional care. The Hospital closed in 1954 and the buildings were converted into a modern school. I was among the final intake: one of the very last foundlings.

I'm sure the children sitting at their desks today in the former Hospital have no idea what ghosts stalk the great building they now occupy. Nor could they imagine the terror of the dormitories – now made into classrooms – and the shocking abuses perpetrated by the older boys after lights out. If there was a single emotion that ruled in those days, it was fear. Fear of the awful bullying that took place at every level; fear of the fierce and humiliating punishments meted out for the slightest misdemeanour; fear of being the weakest in a bare-knuckle fight; fear of what cruel 'game' the dormitory monitor would dream up next to amuse himself. Fear on all sides.

Thankfully we have come a long way since then. The stigma of illegitimacy has disappeared, and with it the financial hardship and the impulse to deny children the warmth and intimacy of family life. My early years, it has to be said, were tough, and there have been many potholes in the road I've travelled since then. It has been difficult to build relationships and trust people, but I feel both humbled and triumphant to be where I am today. As I look at the charmingly old-fashioned inns across the street – the Crown, the Swan and the King's Arms – I think how lovely it would be to bring my family up from Plymouth to stay in one of them for the weekend. When I left the Hospital at fifteen, I could only dream about such things.

In the chapters that follow I will tell my story. It is the story of a boy who spent too many years in an institution where outdated practices did more harm than good. It is also the story of my mother Jean, a desperate woman who felt she had no choice but to give away her firstborn. Growing up afraid and alone in the Foundling Hospital, I used to hope and wish that my mother was out there somewhere, waiting for me.

Miraculously, she was. The moment we rediscovered each other was the happiest moment of my life, and I have taken great pleasure in relating her journey as she described it to me when we finally met each other again. Finding love within the bosom of my real family has helped to heal the wounds inflicted during my childhood. It is, I believe, a story worth telling.

1

Jean

A World in Meltdown

IT WAS A LONG TRAIN JOURNEY from my home in
Scotland to London. I remember the endless thoughts and
emotions swirling around in my head: would my boyfriend
Raymond be at the station to meet me? Would his feelings
have changed in the intervening weeks since we'd last seen
each other? Would he still love me? I was caught between
anxiety and excitement, winding and rewinding strands of
my long red hair around my index finger until they grew
taut and threatened to break. 'My little rosy copperhead'
my mum used to call me in happier times.

It was 1938, the year of Munich and the shameful pact
with Hitler to allow the carving up of Czechoslovakia.
People were nervous about the prospect of another war
and this tension seemed to have cast a dark shadow over
my house. My brother was coming up to military age, after
all. Mother was highly strung at the best of times and lately
she had been erupting like a wild thing. She had never

liked my boyfriends, but her anger towards Raymond and the rows we were having over the relationship were proving impossible to handle.

It had been different with my previous beau, Hugo. He hadn't taken anything seriously: 'frivolous' was the word she used. I can still hear her voice ringing in my ears: 'He might be from a good Protestant family and his father might be the senior partner in one of Glasgow's oldest law firms,' she'd say, 'but he needs to learn his manners and show some respect.' She'd even, unkindly, poke fun at his shortness. Hugo was not, as far as she was concerned, marriage material. We hadn't even talked of marriage, but that didn't stop her sticking her oar in. I think she was getting nervous: I was comfortably into my twenties, and I'm sure she thought it was time I settled down. Hugo had a sunny, happy-go-lucky outlook, he was fun and he made me laugh, but I wasn't too serious about him.

Then came Raymond. He was so different; so intense and earnest, he even wrote verse for me. I never thought I'd fall for someone like him – such a romantic – but he had this charm, this serious sense of devotion that I couldn't resist. We had been introduced by mutual friends. I was twenty-four and he was nineteen, so there was quite an age gap. He must have been conscious of it. His two older sisters certainly thought it was amusing, and when we were out on the town, they would constantly rib him: 'five years this . . .' and 'five years that . . .' He had four siblings altogether and was the youngest, the baby of the family. Like so many in that situation, he was both teased and spoilt.

The strange thing was that my mother treated him quite warmly to begin with. I think she liked his old-world charm and the way he was always immaculately dressed. And he could talk the talk. He had this quiet, refined Glaswegian accent, the one from the posh end of town. It was smooth, like syrup, not like the harsh Lanarkshire brogue we had to listen to every day. A clever boy, he had been privately educated and worked at the Glasgow stock exchange. But then, to her fury, mother found out that he was a Catholic, and an Irish one at that. Even worse, the source of his family wealth was 'the dreaded drink' – the Divers owned one of the city's largest and busiest pubs.

My family, by contrast, was teetotal and my father an elder in the Kirk. We weren't just from different backgrounds; we belonged to different classes, religions, even nations. Sectarian tension was still strong at this time in Scotland, which had been a Protestant country since the Reformation. A flood of Irish Catholic emigrants in the nineteenth century had caused lots of problems, particularly as many were poor and seen as carriers of disease – typhus became known as 'Irish fever'. Many people, including my mother, saw the Irish as drunken, idle and uncivilized – a menace to solid Scottish morals and nationhood.

I couldn't fathom how we were going to make the

relationship work, but although both my parents were against the match, I was convinced that my father would come round in time. Naturally he was unhappy, but he loved me and I felt that if I could prove I was sincere, he would come to accept my decision. My father was a slightly built, mild-mannered man, a pussycat compared with my mother. Taller than her husband, and clever, she was a gifted painter who, I'm sure, would have been quite the bluestocking had she been born in a different time. Instead, domesticity, children and church work made up her life, the only consolation, though an important one, being that she was the absolute governor at home.

Relations between us, never easy, grew increasingly fraught. She seemed to expect the same level of obedience at twenty-four as she had when I was a teenager. After one blistering row, I reached the end of my tether and announced I was leaving. When she'd calmed down, I explained that I would head for London where production was picking up and jobs, if not abundant, were at least rising, which was not the case in the depression-hit North. To my astonishment, she raised no objections; she even said that it might do me good – broaden my horizons and all that. I suspected the real reason she wanted me to go was because it would put an end to my relationship with Raymond.

We faced opposition on all sides. Raymond's mother Sarah – even more of a matriarch than mine – was also against the union. I'm sure she saw me as some sort of scarlet woman, snaring and corrupting her darling boy with all my years of 'experience' as she saw them. She was a formidable adversary, a powerful woman who ran her business and her home with an iron fist. I suppose she had no choice: her husband, Johnnie, was far too fond of the bottle for a publican. By closing time, he was so out of it that he could rarely string two words together, so although he was a fine fellow and a generous host to his friends, he was a disaster to his family. Raymond once told me of the shame he felt as a young boy, watching through the curtains as a taxi brought his parents home, his mother supporting her drunken husband across the pavement and into the house. It was a fine, big house in a posh area, and Raymond knew that the neighbours, who already took a dim view of the Irish, would enjoy having their prejudices confirmed. His mother, who was from rural Donegal, had worked hard to raise her family's fortunes, and was proud that profits from the pub had provided the big house, private education for the children and a new fur coat whenever needed, so it was with anger that Raymond saw his father cast them back towards the gutter. He worshipped his mother; but he ended up despising his father.

I knew this and had had to tread carefully. Raymond loved me, certainly, but I couldn't be sure how much – and in a head-to-head against his mother, I didn't know whose side he would take. However, it seemed we wanted the same thing. We hatched a plan to escape our families and their rigid values that would see us journeying to set up a new life in South Africa, where, with a bit of luck, we would make our fortune. Raymond was to go on ahead, get himself established and then call for me to join him. In the meantime, I would find a job in London and try to put a little money aside for the future. Neither his mother nor mine knew of our crafty machinations. Indeed, Raymond's mother thought he was going alone, and she was so keen to prevent a change of heart and to ensure he stayed away from me that she set up a bank account in Cape Town and deposited some funds there.

But as the train rumbled on through the rainy November landscape, I couldn't help but worry we'd been too impulsive. What if I couldn't find work? I'd had a good job for seven years in Glasgow as a legal secretary in a small friendly office, but the legal systems of England and Scotland were so different that I would have to look for a new type of role. I consoled myself that I was a skilled typist and knew shorthand, so surely there would be something. London, after all, was a big city, the largest in the world so Raymond had told me, and I started to believe him as the train reached suburbia and slowly threaded its way through the jungle of houses and flats, shops and roads. The journey to the centre took a long time. Compared with Glasgow, London seemed colossal. Houses without end.

Finally the train juddered and came to a halt. Every door flew open and the passengers, so sedate minutes ago, jumped into action, frantically shrugging on coats and collecting all manner of cases and trunks. As they poured out of the carriages and onto the platform, flowing at speed towards the ticket barrier, I found it all a bit unnerving. How would I cope if such manic behaviour was the norm in London? And where was Raymond? I searched among the sea of faces beyond the barrier for the only one guaranteed to calm my anxieties. The crush was so great that I lost my footing and was carried forward, and then, to my relief, I saw him. He was smiling and waving and suddenly I felt better. I was not alone in this crazy hubbub of a world; he was there, waiting for me, preparing our future. As I passed through the barrier he pushed his way forward, enveloped me in a big bear hug and lifted me clean off my feet before kissing me passionately.

'Hi, Jeannie,' he breathed into my ear, his arms still wrapped tightly around me. I was quite taken aback. I'd never experienced such open and uninhibited emotion from him before. It was a bit embarrassing, but lovely at the same time. I had been so worried about seeing him again, and here he was, my still gorgeous boy, just as much in love with me as I was with him. If this was the effect of London life, I thought to myself, then I could be happy here.

I wondered later whether such warmth was partly caused

by the anonymity of the capital. Perhaps Raymond felt he could express his feelings openly in London because there was no chance his activities would be reported back to his mother. There was also the added bonus that no one knew about our age difference – here we looked just like any other young couple in love.

It was wonderful to feel so free about our relationship at last, but I did feel a touch of Presbyterian guilt as I knew we would be passing ourselves off as man and wife. I think Raymond might have felt the same way. He seemed ever so slightly nervous when he took my hand at the station and said, 'I've got us a nice little place. It's not quite the Ritz, but it'll do. You'll approve, Jeannie.' He suggested stopping off at a Lyons teashop before heading to our lodgings, which we did – and I very much enjoyed my large cup of milky tea and the toasted crumpets with pooling butter. It was as if he wanted to show me that I meant something to him, that I was his girl, his wife-to-be, and not some love-struck, naive lass to be taken advantage of at the first opportunity.

He couldn't have known how thrilled I was by the prospect of our own home, but I'm sure he got an inkling the moment we entered the flat. I felt such a wave of joy that I couldn't resist leaping onto the bed and jumping up and down in excitement. Raymond followed, wrestling me down and holding my arms fast above my head. I put up a perfunctory show of resistance before submitting quite happily, not for the first time.

The following morning I awoke with a terrible feeling of sadness that this new chapter of our lives would be so brief. I looked at Raymond, sleeping so soundly, and ran my finger lightly along his cheek. I knew I would feel utterly desolate without him. He had told me the night before that his ship sailed in two months. I had been hoping to spend longer in our London flat, and dreaded the aching loneliness that was to come. I stroked his face again, bending to give him a kiss. His eyes opened lazily and he looked up, smiling.

'What's for today, Jeannie? Is it the tourist trail?'

I frowned. 'I don't think so. Listen to the rain on the windows.' Moving across the room, I pulled back the curtains to prove my point.

'Maybe it's for the best,' Raymond said with a cheeky wink. 'I fancy a lazy day with my woman. What about doing me a nice breakfast?'

I was only too happy to oblige and set about preparing eggs, thick buttered toast and steaming cups of tea. It was my first taste at playing his wife and I loved it.

The day passed quickly as we talked about our plans for the future and our happiness at escaping the arguments at home. The truth was we were rather gleeful – almost childishly so – imagining how our mothers, in far away Scotland, would be congratulating themselves at having engineered a split that would prove fatal. How wrong they were going to be!

The following days were almost dreamlike. We took romantic strolls through London's parks and couldn't quite believe how many and how extensive they were. To have such spaces in the centre of a city, untouched by the industrial revolution, was a marvel. I also liked the little leafy squares that were dotted everywhere, and, indeed, seemed to pop up when you least expected them, as you were rounding a corner or walking down an alleyway. If it wasn't for the thick smog that came from the coal-fuelled power stations and domestic fires, London would have been a perfect city.

Raymond was so good to me during this period. He'd take me out in the evenings, to the theatre or for meals in smart little restaurants. At the time I wondered how any future honeymoon could match this blissful interlude. But underneath the joy, there was the dark, looming threat of separation.

All too soon the morning I had been dreading arrived. I woke up but kept my eyes firmly closed, knowing that as soon as I opened them I would see Raymond's two bulging bags by the door. I wasn't ready for him to go. The sky was overcast and rain clouds were threatening as we made our way to Waterloo station. Ominous weather for an ominous occasion, I thought. We caught the train to

Southampton, but the journey was in total contrast to the one I had made just two months earlier. Few words passed between us, each of us sunk in our own private gloom.

At the quayside, amongst all the happy faces and the waving and calling of messages of luck to loved ones, all I felt was desolation, while Raymond clasped me in a tight embrace until the final call came for passengers to board.

Tears welled in both our eyes, but I couldn't hold back and began to sob uncontrollably. With a final kiss, he pulled himself away and hurried up the gangplank before disappearing from sight. He didn't turn round, which was just as well. Had he done so, he would have seen the full depth of my misery as I crumbled inside.

My return to London was miserable. Heavy rain fell from the swollen clouds, and I arrived back at the flat wet through and utterly bereft. Our home for two months, a place that had been so full of laughter and joy, was now stricken with an unbearable sadness. I knew that I wouldn't be able to stay on with so many memories of what we had shared and lost, so I left the very next morning and spent the rest of the day looking for a suitable alternative. I found a neat little end-of-terrace house in Hampstead with a couple of rooms to let and shared bathrooms. The landlady was a widow from the late war and she seemed pleased by the prospect of some younger company.

With funds starting to run low, I knew it was urgent

now that I find a job. Although I had been rather half-hearted in searching while Raymond was around, there were numerous vacancies advertised – column after column – and I set about applying for as many of these as I could.

But the loss of Raymond had caused an ache that just wouldn't go away. And there was something else that had been worrying me for some time. I had missed a few periods. The first had gone past while I was still living with my parents, and I had told myself that it was to be expected, given the stress at home and the excitement of planning for South Africa. But when a second month passed with no result, and then a third, I knew I should see a doctor. Tests followed and within a short time the news that I had been dreading was confirmed. I was pregnant and, with Raymond gone, utterly alone.

There was nobody I could turn to. All my friends were hundreds of miles away and the thought of going home and having to face my mother sent a shiver down my spine. I considered telling my warm-hearted landlady, whom I was getting to know quite well, but I simply couldn't take the risk of being asked to leave. It seemed like a hopeless situation, but I knew that I couldn't surrender to despair. I had to stay strong. I agonized about whether or not I should tell Raymond, but with all the difficulties he was experiencing trying to find a job in South Africa, it wasn't the right time; I didn't want to add to his worries when they were already so great. It never crossed my mind to have a termination. How could I? They were against the law, carried out by backstreet operators with unhygienic implements and dangerous pills. Besides, this was our baby, mine and Raymond's, and I knew that such a betrayal would stay with me to my dying day.

In the midst of all this anxiety, I was finally offered a job. It was in a busy export office and I took an instant liking to the woman who ran the operation. A spinster in her middle years, Muriel was smartly if severely dressed, usually in brown tweed, a starched cotton shirt and round-toed Oxfords. She was careerist and, it has to be said, somewhat intimidating. One of the girls in the office referred to her as 'old hatchet face', but I found her to be the nicest, most caring person I would ever meet. From day one, for reasons I never fully understood, she took a special, even motherly, interest in me. Maybe she had an inkling that – far away from home – I was in need of a friend.

But I had lied, albeit by omission, to get the job, and this played on my conscience. At the time of interview I had felt that there was no other way, since no employer would have taken me on knowing that I was pregnant and would have to leave in five months' time – to go where, I still had no clue.

I had been raised in a religious household, and all these lies and the shame of finding myself pregnant began to take their toll. As the weeks passed and Muriel's many kindnesses accrued, I knew I would have to tell her. I worried myself sick about it, imagining the terrible scene and how my mentor would feel when she realized that I'd let her down. As nice as she was, I was conscious that she had been with the firm all her working life and would feel duty-bound to tell her superiors. Such a revelation would bring instant dismissal.

However, when I finally summoned the courage to confide the truth about my situation, Muriel's response was astonishing. She didn't rant or rail or order me off the premises as I'm sure many in her position would have done. Instead she took my hand and looked at me with such concern that I burst into tears. Sweeping me up into her arms, and stroking the back of my head, she whispered, 'You poor, poor child.'

The tightness of her hug almost took my breath away. She smoothed the hair away from my tear-stained face and plucked a handkerchief from her pocket. 'Don't tell anyone else about this,' she said. 'This must be kept strictly between the two of us. No one else is to know. Do you understand?'

I nodded, and from that moment, Muriel, who had taken me under her wing from the first, became my guardian angel. She was so considerate and took an interest in every aspect of my well-being, asking how I was sleeping and eating and whether I needed any rest breaks during the day. She was one of life's true gems, and I only wished I'd told her sooner. Needless to say, my position in the firm remained secure.

2

Jean

The Man Who Loved Children

I<small>T</small> <small>WAS</small> M<small>URIEL</small> <small>WHO</small> <small>TOLD</small> <small>ME</small> about the Foundling Hospital. I had explained from the outset that it wasn't possible to keep my baby. Raymond was on the other side of the world, we were not yet married, and I didn't have the means to support a child on my own.

The charity sounded marvellous: a wealthy, benevolent organization that would take my baby and bring him or her up in the countryside. I grew quite excited about the idea of fresh air instead of the cloying smog that on some days was so thick you couldn't even see your feet. But undoubtedly the best thing about the scheme was that it needn't be a permanent adoption. The Hospital would provide care and an education, giving my little one the start in life that I could not, but once Raymond and I had set ourselves up, we could reclaim our child. Or so I thought at the time.

My heart sank a little when Muriel told me that the

application process and vetting procedures were complex. It seemed that the governors adhered to strict policies that had been honed over two hundred years and would only accept babies from what they considered to be 'good' girls with firm morals who had been unlucky, let down or taken advantage of in some way. Careless or loose women they were not interested in.

I wondered at the seeming unfairness of this policy, since whatever the shortcomings of the mothers, their babies were entirely innocent, but the capacity of the Hospital was limited and the governors had learned from their past mistakes: admitting too many children compromised the level of care they could provide and often led to outbreaks of disease. The governors also wanted to ensure that the women were – in their eyes – worthy, and that given a second chance they would use it wisely. For this reason, the mother's prospects were assessed alongside the needs of her child. I felt that I had become pregnant through misfortune. I also considered myself to be in a stable and loving relationship with a decent man, and I thought I deserved a second chance. But what if the governors didn't take that view? What if they didn't think I had met their criteria? What if they thought I was a loose woman, one who had brought it on herself?

Muriel tried to calm these anxieties. She phoned the charity headquarters in Bloomsbury, and in her quiet and professional manner made some notes for us to look over.

The process, it was clear, would be extremely rigorous. I would have to write a detailed letter explaining how I came to find myself in such a hopeless situation. No information was to be withheld. They would need to know how long I had known the father; the circumstances in which we had met; how our relationship had developed; both our family histories; my future plans – some of which I hadn't even worked out for myself yet.

I was reluctant to give any information about my parents as I had been hoping to keep my pregnancy a secret from them, at least for the time being. They would be upset and disappointed to learn about the baby and the fact that I had defied their wishes and rekindled my romance with Raymond. It made me feel sick to think about how they might react. But I was beginning to realize the path I had chosen was not going to be an easy one. If my application was to be considered seriously, then the officials at the Hospital would need to check out my story and my character, which might involve talking to my parents.

Muriel was very supportive and helped me realize that I couldn't sweep the whole matter under the carpet. My parents were far away but they would have to know, especially as I would want to reclaim my child as soon as Raymond and I were settled in a home of our own. Muriel also pointed out that the Foundling Hospital was a strongly Christian charity and it wouldn't hurt to reveal that my father was an elder in the Kirk. After giving careful thought to my letter, and helped by Muriel, I sent it off and waited anxiously for a reply.

Those days of waiting were the longest days I had ever known. But then came the reply I had prayed for: they wanted to see me.

I got up early on the morning of the meeting, and feeling very nervous, looked at myself in the mirror for a long time. Muriel had advised me to dress well but a little soberly, as though I was going to take the stand in court, which, in a way, I was. I'd selected a long navy woollen skirt and a cream blouse with a lace collar and pearl buttons. It was my Sunday best, the smartest outfit I owned. As I brushed my hair, I wondered whether I should pin it up or not. I was more comfortable with it down, but would red waves suggest coquettishness? I decided to let it down. I wasn't a loose woman and it was my job to make them see that.

When I arrived at the Hospital's head office in Brunswick Square, despite seeing Muriel's friendly face waiting for me, my heart began to race. It was a stylish neo-Georgian building of very recent construction. I'd never been anywhere quite so posh. The lobby was lined with resplendent portraits of all the great men who had been governors in the past, some austere, some kindly, but all somehow sitting in judgement. The charity had always received strong support from the arts, and the Hospital owned works by Gainsborough, Reynolds and Hogarth.

They must have been worth a fortune, and I remember thinking how kind and generous – in those cruel and uncaring times – those men were to safeguard the future of so many helpless children.

The interview was set for eleven o'clock, and I started to feel more and more nervous as I watched the hands on the great grandfather clock move around. The ticks sounded thunderous in the semi-darkness of the silent hall. I was so relieved that Muriel had insisted on coming with me. We shared an occasional hushed word, but even this felt somehow wrong, as if we were breaking some unspoken covenant to sit and reflect on what I'd brought about.

My demeanour must have reflected my mood of deep apprehension because Muriel took my hand and whispered that it was all going to be all right. Each word was amplified by the oak panelling on the walls and the polished parquet floor. More minutes passed and the silence grew oppressive. My thoughts circled round and round the sorts of questions that would be thrown at me and how I should respond. I hoped and prayed that they wouldn't be too personal, too intimate.

Suddenly, there was a loud creak and a door opened. Sharp, resounding footsteps made their way towards us.

'Miss Craig?' enquired a female voice. I looked up with a weak half-smile, feeling a sudden snag of guilt at what I imagined to be a heavy emphasis on the 'Miss'. 'Would you like to come this way?'

I stood up and cast an almost pleading backward glance at Muriel, who had also risen to her feet.

'Only Miss Craig,' said the woman.

I followed her along the hall and up the imposing timber staircase, clutching gratefully at the handrail as my legs had become suddenly unsteady.

The woman stopped in front of a large oak door and knocked twice. I couldn't hear the reply but I guess it must have been affirmative as she briskly pushed it open and walked through. I followed and found myself in a long, gallery-like room with the largest table I had ever seen running down the centre. It was wooden, like everything else, with a top polished like glass. I had assumed I would be talking to a woman, perhaps with a nurse there, but to my consternation and shock I saw eight middle-aged or elderly men sitting in a line along one side of the table. Facing them, in the middle on the other side, was a single empty chair. The woman beckoned me towards it and one of the men invited me to sit down. His voice, at least, was kindly. I felt shaky. I'm sure I was trembling. Only at this point did it dawn on me that I was before the board of governors.

I moved quickly into my seat, keeping my eyes down as I did so. A glass of water had been placed in front of me and the same kindly voice told me to help myself when I felt the need. I saw that there were no other glasses on the table.

The whole situation struck me as surreal and the interview that followed was the strangest I would ever experience. Though the questions were wide-ranging and some might say intrusive, they were asked in such a matter-of-fact and fatherly way – almost in the tone of a family doctor – that I found no difficulty or embarrassment in answering them. During periods when my interviewers were murmuring between themselves, I studied the room with its pastel-green walls, covered with old masters, its intricately moulded white rococo ceiling, and marvellously sculpted fireplace facing the windows. It was quite the most beautiful room I had ever been in.

Three-quarters of an hour had passed – though it felt like double this – when one of my inquisitors, the man opposite me, who seemed to be in charge, drew his associates into a huddle. Shortly after this, he announced that they needn't detain me any longer. He thanked me for my patience and for being so forthcoming, and then ushered me towards the door with a smile, which I returned.

Considering how much I had agonized before the meeting, I felt it had gone well and that I had acquitted myself at least satisfactorily, but still the days that followed were anxious ones. I wondered whether I should have spoken more boldly at times, been less reticent or even pleaded with them for help.

The thought of what I would do if I were turned down was unbearable. Raymond had gone and I still hadn't admitted my situation to my parents. There was no way I could return to their house one day with a baby. Muriel had mentioned adoption – she didn't fully understand how much Raymond and I loved each other – but the idea of losing my baby forever was one that I didn't want to contemplate. I clung to the idea that my child would be accepted by the Foundling Hospital and that Raymond and I would reclaim him or her once we had set ourselves up in South Africa.

Fortunately the wait was not a long one. A letter arrived explaining that the Hospital would take my child and give me the breathing space I had longed for. Looking back, it's hard to grasp how happy that letter made me feel. If I'd known then that I was to be separated from my baby for twenty years, I might have torn that precious letter to shreds.

I received another letter several weeks later, in which my mother revealed that an official called Mr Long had been to visit her and my father in Glasgow. He had told them about the pregnancy and had also talked to Raymond's parents, my old boss at the law firm, my family doctor, and even Raymond's best friend. Though I had been made aware that the Hospital would look into my background, the scale of the investigation surprised me. I could very well imagine how incensed Raymond's mother would be to hear of the pregnancy. As for my own mother, she was clearly shocked and saddened by the turn of events and wrote that it wasn't the future she had wanted for me. But there was none of the fury I had been expecting, and she ended the note by wishing me well and saying that she would be thinking of me in the months ahead. I had no real sense of my father's views but the letter gave me hope that I would be able to go home when it was all over.

I wrote regularly to Raymond, assuring him that I was well and happy with my new work, but I never once mentioned my condition. I didn't want to burden him with news of my pregnancy, and I felt sure that his parents, having never liked me, would not let on in case he came rushing back. His own letters were warm and full of longing to see me, but they also spoke of his difficulties in finding a permanent job. Until he had achieved this, it was clear he was in no position to ask me to join him. This was getting him down, and I spent many lines trying to reassure him that he should take his time. I could and would wait it out until he called for me.

The rest of my pregnancy ran smoothly. I didn't put on much weight and I found that it was quite easy to conceal my bump under a thick jumper. If my colleagues noticed, they didn't say anything. I left the office a couple of months before I was due to give birth and waited nervously for my baby to arrive. I hoped that the labour wouldn't be too painful but I really didn't know what to expect and I wished there was someone – a friend or close relative – who I could talk to about it. Although I was in touch with my parents, they hadn't offered to visit me and I didn't feel able to ask my mother about her experience. But it was an exciting time as well as a nervous one and my thoughts turned to names; I didn't know whether I was expecting a boy or a girl so I made a list for both.

I gave birth to a healthy boy on 14 May 1939 at the Royal Free Hospital in London. He was beautiful and I fell in love the very first moment I saw him. Muriel was close by throughout and it was a great comfort to have her there, especially as the attending doctor invited twelve medical students to see my baby into the world. As the child of a conservative, church-going family, I would in other circumstances never have agreed, but in the middle of labour – emotional and exhausted – I found that it was the least of my concerns who saw me. And everyone else faded into the background when the baby was placed in my arms. He had the most delicate skin – soft, pinkish and warm – and his fingers and toes were so tiny, I could barely believe they were real. I knew that I would have to be very gentle with him, and those first few days, I kept checking with the nurses to make sure I was holding him in the right way.

The Foundling Hospital allowed mothers to nurse their infants for several weeks as they thought this was the best way to build up the child's immunity. I treasured the period we spent in the special mother and baby home in the St

John's Wood district of London and I found myself becoming more and more attached to my son, whom I named Derek, with every day that went by. I began to think of him as my own and dreaded the moment when I would have to hand him over, knowing that the loss, when it came, would be crushing. During those few weeks, I made friends among the other mothers whose children were also to pass into the care of the Hospital, including one very special friend, Doris, who would remain part of my life for ever after. We filled our days with laughter and strolls in the park, our babies gurgling away as we pushed them along in the early summer sunshine.

Then one day, when Derek was nine weeks old, I was informed that I would need to make the half-hour journey to the Brunswick Square headquarters of the Foundling Hospital with my baby, for a number of 'routine' checks to be carried out. Muriel agreed to accompany me and we thought we might find somewhere for a spot of tea afterwards. I started to fret and feel as anxious as I had when I had been waiting for my interview seven months before – again there was that overpowering silence, but this time it was relieved by the baby's occasional cries.

A nurse appeared and asked if she could borrow Derek for a minute – weighing purposes, she said. She returned shortly, pronouncing him to be a 'bonnie boy' and tweaking what she described as his 'button nose' before giving him back to me. Twice more I handed over my tiny son, who by this point was wide awake and beaming at all the fuss being made of him. First it was for 'blood tests' and then because the nurse said that the doctor had arrived and wanted to see him. This time, minutes passed, followed by more minutes. Half an hour went by. Muriel took my hand and squeezed it tightly as the dreadful realization came upon us that this was it. Tears filled my eyes. I began to rock backwards and forwards, clasping my face with both hands as sobs shook through my body. Muriel placed an arm around my back and drew me into her, but it didn't help. I was beyond all human help. It felt like my guardian angels had deserted me.

A man appeared in front of us in a white coat and introduced himself as the doctor. He cleared his throat and looked down at me with pity in his eyes. 'You'll be pleased to know that you have a very healthy boy. He's absolutely fine, in every respect. However, I think you know it's time. The Hospital has to assume its agreed responsibilities. You know he will forever be in safe hands.' I closed my eyes. My heart had skipped a beat at his use of the word 'forever'.

'I'm very sorry, but it's for the best. You know that,' he added softly, in a barely discernible whisper. Then he turned away.

It was, without doubt, a procedure best left to a man. The Foundling Hospital had long ago discovered that few women could be persuaded to, or could indeed cope with, such a heartbreaking assignment.

3

Jean

Into a Dark Place

THE SUMMER OF 1939 was not one that I would forget in a hurry. I had lost my baby and the world was about to lose its peace. The mood was one of deep foreboding and everyone seemed certain there would be another global conflict, another young generation of men lost to the calamity of war.

A blanket of despondency also descended over my personal life. Raymond had not had much luck in South Africa and so he moved north into the Rhodesias (present-day Zambia and Zimbabwe). Letters became less and less frequent as he moved deeper into the African bush looking for the opportunity that had eluded him further south. I could at least console myself that the letters were still coming, though I began to miss him more than ever and felt very alone with my family so far away. I also missed my baby boy. I tried so hard not to grieve for him, telling myself that he was still there and this was only a temporary solution, one that I had opted for, after all. Nights were the worst. Once I'd finished work, made dinner, washed up and written to Raymond, I couldn't seem to keep the pretence up any longer and I'd cry myself to sleep, hoping my landlady wouldn't hear.

Then the catastrophe that everyone was dreading happened. On 3 September Britain declared war on Germany, and by the end of the month sandbags were being piled high outside government buildings all over London and people started applying sticky tape to every window. Suddenly the streets were full of men in uniform, and a surprising number of women too. To cap it all, the beautiful parks that I so admired were being dug up to install massive anti-aircraft guns – sacrilege, I thought. The blackout was enforced every evening, and I despaired as the lights of the capital were extinguished, plunging us all into gloom. Accidents on the streets, many fatal, rocketed, and life became very grim as we awaited the onslaught of bombs.

I had never liked the autumn – the chilly nights and browning leaves, a sign of the long hard winter months to come – but that autumn left me feeling a deep melancholy. Phone calls from my parents became more strident as they reminded me of my solemn promise to return in the event of war. I was torn between not wanting to distance myself from my baby and from the prospect of joining Raymond – which was easier to cling to in London – and the duty

I owed to my parents. On top of that I had also to consider my own well-being: my heart ached every time I saw a mother with her baby in the street. These terrible times made me long for home. I agonized over what to do. At the end of September, having received only a single letter from Raymond in the entire month, I took the decision to return north. I wrote to Raymond telling him how fraught life had become in the capital and how much pressure my parents were putting me under – and I begged him to understand.

The journey back to Glasgow and home to East Kilbride reminded me of the one I had made to Southampton. There was no joy, no wonderful feeling of excitement at starting a new life; only dreadful uncertainty.

I knew that for my baby, Derek, the opposite would be the case. Certainty would govern every stage of development in his young life. It would all be mapped out. First, he would be given a new name. Then he would be placed with foster parents in the country, where he would spend his early years before joining the main school in Berkhamsted at the age of four or five. From that point he would grow up among the other similarly placed children, all of whom would have to learn to call the institution home.

I tried not to think too much about the Hospital. I knew that it would be a cold, impersonal place where he would receive little affection. During my interview, I learned that basic instruction would be given in reading, writing, religion and numeracy, all of which were deemed valuable for the working classes. There was one exception to this list: music. When George Frideric Handel had been a governor in the eighteenth century, he had given a benefit concert every year in the Hospital chapel to raise funds for the charity, and had even composed the Foundling Hospital anthem, 'Blessed are they that considereth the poor', which borrowed from his earlier works and included the 'Hallelujah' chorus from *Messiah*. Ever since then, music had been afforded a special place, and I was told many of the boys sang in the choir and went on to join the ranks of military bands.

But while knowing all this cheered me a little, I never lost sight of my intention to reclaim Derek before he joined the school, and I was far more concerned with his immediate future – and his foster parents. The Foundling Hospital wouldn't give me any details about Derek or his location, but I knew there was a tradition of housing the foundlings within a small group of towns just outside the capital, including Chertsey, Addlestone and Saffron Walden.

I found myself thinking a lot about the woman who would be cradling my baby, wiping away his tears and rocking him to sleep every night. I'd heard that the foster mothers were chosen carefully. They were not to be educated women but rather the best of the working class, as there was little point in the children growing up in homes where they might start to think above their station. I needed to believe Derek's new mother would be kind and maternal, but would she come to love him as much as I had – as I did still? Would he take to her immediately or would he miss me? Would he remember how I'd held him in my arms, how I'd kissed his plump cheek? I yearned for him and a part of me hoped that he might feel my absence, and yet I prayed that he would adapt and enjoy the warmth and closeness of family life wherever he was. It was a difficult time and I felt demolished by my loss.

4

Tom

Keep the Home Fires Burning

THE NEW HOME that was found for me was, as my mother suspected, in Saffron Walden, one of the little market towns north of London. An historic town with buildings dating from the medieval period set in lovely rolling countryside, it was known as the jewel of Essex and was a marvellous place to grow up. I can still recall the sweet smell of the saffron crocus, almost like honey with a hint of the sea. My second mum Elsie used to call them 'flowers with golden spice', and to dissuade me from picking any she'd tell me stories about how the flower contained a magical extract which had been used to create rich perfumes and medicine since the middle ages. The flower was so important, so precious, that it had given the town its name. I was an impish child, always on the lookout to cause some mischief or other, but I never picked a single flower.

Elsie wasn't strictly my second mum; she was my third,

not that I knew this at the time. After I had been weaned by my real mother, the Foundling Hospital had placed me with a Saffron woman by the name of Ada. She already had two children of her own and found looking after me very hard work. I wouldn't sleep for more than two hours at a time and was an irritable, grouchy little thing, always crying and prone to an upset stomach. After two months Ada was at the end of her tether.

'My, oh my!' she moaned one day to her friend Elsie. 'I can't go on like this, honest I can't. I'm getting no rest. It takes an hour to get the little tyke off to sleep and then he wakes up after no time at all. You were so lucky with your Janet, sweet thing that she is. But this is no reward for taking on a foundling baby. I'm going to have to give him back.'

As Elsie listened to her friend's lament, a thought began to form. She had already taken in a foundling the year before and loved her to bits. Janet was now eighteen months old and her own daughter, Monica, was almost three. Maybe it was time to add another to her happy brood.

'No, no, you can't do that,' Elsie remonstrated with her friend. 'Give him to me. I'll sort him out.'

'Are you sure? Do you really think you could?' asked the incredulous but somewhat relieved Ada.

'Of course I can – and I really will! Besides, it'll be a nice little surprise for Cecil.'

'Oh, it'll be that, all right,' laughed Ada. 'But are you

sure? Are you really, really sure? Do you think the Hospital will agree to it?'

'Of course they will, and what's more, Cecil's always wanted a boy,' said Elsie, and that was that.

Elsie, luckily, was made of sterner stuff than Ada, and with the help of her husband Cecil, who took turns with her through the long nights, she struggled through to calmer waters. It was later discovered that I was allergic to dairy products, and the bad temper which Ada had put down to my difficult nature was the result of near-permanent gripes. I've often wondered whether such an allergy would have developed if I'd been able to stay with my mother and been breastfed for longer.

Both Elsie and Cecil were very happy when I came along. They were a proper family – and Cecil had his boy at last, a little sandy-haired one with blue eyes. I was a marked contrast to my fellow foundling, Janet, with her deep brown eyes and her beautiful jet-black wavy hair. She was a tiny thing, smaller than me even though she was eighteen months older, and blessed with the sweetest of natures. I was a scamp by comparison. Monica, the eldest and the natural child of the family, was a tomboy and, like me, always getting into hot water. She was a very large girl for her age, clearly taking after her mother who stood six feet tall in her slippers – a phenomenal height for that time.

Elsie was a salt-of-the-earth Saffron woman: robust,

forthright and cheerful. She had a great sense of humour and laughed a lot. She was twenty-six when she took me in, and, although not exactly beautiful, had a handsome figure. My dad used to tease that all the men in Saffron were after her, which made him the 'luckiest man in town'. After they'd married and had Monica, Elsie couldn't seem to conceive again which caused much disappointment for the pair, but they were a lovely, big-hearted couple and when Elsie suggested they volunteer to look after one of the little babies from the colony that seemed to have descended from the Foundling Hospital, Cecil leapt at the idea. The years I spent in their care were happy ones and I believe this positive stamp stayed with me, increasing my resilience and helping me survive what was to come.

Home was a small mid-terrace cottage with the name Alpha Place. It had a tiny garden backing onto a large buttercupped field where cows were often to be seen grazing and rabbits were in abundance. No time in my childhood would ever be so idyllic. Cecil was a kind man who, along with his towering wife, treated me as if I was his own. He liked to keep ferrets and would often take us rabbiting for extra meat during the tight rationing of the war.

My fascination with the ferrets was great, and I had to be constantly told not to put my tiny fingers through the wires of the cage.

'You'll lose them if you go on like that,' warned my dad. 'They'll bite them clean off.'

I looked at my fingers – they did seem very small so maybe Dad was right. But then I looked at the furry creatures and felt sorely tempted. Cecil wisely placed a hand around my chest and pulled me away.

I can't begin to describe the excitement we three kids felt when Dad would release a ferret into the rabbit's warren. Down the ferret would go into one hole and out the rabbit would come from another. Dad would be waiting with his sack as both animals came rocketing out at breakneck speed, hurtling headlong into the sack. He would then bravely plunge his arm in to retrieve the now manic ferret before it tore the rabbit apart, taking a big risk, given the ferret's rampant bloodlust and the fact that it couldn't distinguish between owner and prey in the darkness of the sack. Those trips were action-packed and deeply thrilling. I loved every minute.

Life for us three kids was an outdoor one. We didn't like to spend much time in the cottage as it was cramped and very dark, but I didn't mind so much during the winter months when snow lay all around, as the cottage's smallness made it seem cosier. Father used to keep the cottage warm by burning wood. I loved the crack and sizzle of a new log being thrown onto the grate, and to this day the earthy smell of burning wood brings back my favourite memories of those long-ago winters.

There always seemed to be an endless supply of logs.

We never needed to use coal, which was just as well as it was in short supply with wartime rationing. Cecil was not only lucky to work on a farm but even luckier to have a good relationship with the farmer. A veteran of the First World War, the farmer was lame from a shrapnel wound and very chesty after being gassed in the trenches, and my father became his right-hand man, taking care of all the heavy jobs he couldn't manage. As a way to say thanks, the farmer used to let him collect firewood from the land as well as take home an extra sack of potatoes or a few extra vegetables and the odd cut of meat now and then, so we didn't fare too badly.

I used to go out with Dad on his foraging trips and would stand and watch as he sawed through massive tree trunks before cleaving the logs into four with his axe.

'Let me have a go, Dad,' I pleaded with him one bright but chilly morning. He looked quite serious for a moment and then gave me the long-handled axe. But as I strained to lift it above my knee, he grabbed it away from me laughing.

'Don't get ahead of yourself, Tommy boy,' he said. 'Your day will come. You'll probably end up bigger than me.'

Like most fathers, when there was a distance to go he would hoist me up on his shoulders, and sometimes he would run scarily fast over the rough ground of the farm to get back home. Once he took a tumble and we both fell headlong into a hedgerow, which luckily broke our fall.

It was a hawthorn and he had to sit there for a minute or two afterwards gingerly plucking thorns out of his hair and clothes, but as I'd gone shooting over the top of the hedge, I didn't get prickled. He swore me to keep our tumble a secret and not tell Mum or even the girls.

'As sure as God made little apples,' Dad said, 'those girls will spill the beans and let on, and then your mummy will be mad at me.'

I didn't split on him, but he got his comeuppance a couple of weeks later when he once again hoisted me up onto his shoulders. I loved being so close to him and seeing the world from a great height, but entering the cottage that evening he didn't bend down far enough and whacked my head on the low arch of the doorway. No real harm was done, though Mum thought otherwise.

'Come here, my babe,' she cried when she heard me howling and saw a thin trickle of blood on my forehead. 'What has Daddy done to you, what has he done?'

The bump didn't take long to heal, which was just as well because Dad was squarely in the doghouse until it did.

The girls used to take more pleasure in staying with Mum at home, although they would come out and play sometimes. For me it was the farm, always the farm. It was there that I discovered the pastime which would get me into so much trouble later on – climbing trees. Cecil and Elsie kept a close eye on me at all times, ensuring that my ambitions didn't run away with me, and would only let me onto the small ones with low boughs – and even then I was never allowed to climb much higher than shoulder height, where they could catch me if I fell.

Haystacks ran a close second where entertainment was concerned. Nowadays you don't see haystacks of the sort we used to play in. All those perfectly compressed sausage-like bales covered in black plastic and dotted all over the fields are, I suppose, an improvement in terms of health and safety, but there's no way they can be as exciting. Our haystacks were the size and shape of houses, and if there was plenty of hay at the lower levels you could jump down from a great height without risk of injury. It was huge fun, as was covering ourselves in masses of it and waiting to be found in a game of hide and seek. We were always slinging great bundles of the stuff at each other, as much as our arms could hold.

Harvest was a very special time of year. All of us kids would join the effort, clutching a rake or other implement and trying to copy the actions of our parents (although in reality we'd spend most of the time hurling ourselves into and off the great piles of hay). After their hard work, the adults would retire to the Pig & Whistle pub and we'd cool our heels outside with a soft drink and a packet of crisps. It was a riotous occasion, full of laughter and lots of back-slapping. Walking home with heavy legs and drowsy eyes, we'd breathe in the rich camomile-like smell of the silage and know that all was well in the world.

It was strange to feel this degree of peace considering I grew up in a world of war. It began when I was three months old and raged on until I was six. Everything was subordinated to it, just everything. And yet there was this other world, a world which my foster parents created for us in their little cottage. It was a world of love and security, into which ugliness was very rarely allowed to intrude.

There was one notable exception, although I didn't see it as ugliness at the time. It was my earliest memory – of a burning bomber attempting to make a crash landing. I can only have been two or three, but the shock of the event burned it into my consciousness so that I can still remember it vividly today. Large parts of the landscape I grew up in were uniformly flat as far as the eye could see and perfect bomber country. It was close to the great bulge of the Norfolk Broads and the fenland to the north which, over the centuries, had been drained and reclaimed from the sea, and across its broad expanses, dozens of airfields were laid down to facilitate the long runways which the bombers, once loaded with their heavy cargo, required in order to lift into the air. From these perfectly positioned east-facing plains, our boys would take the fight to the enemy.

There may have been parts of rural England which were

not hives of wartime activity, but not here. We were in the thick of it. Bombers roared across our skies every day, and we always knew when a big raid was in the offing because the numbers would swell into the hundreds. It was not the mighty rumble of the engine – a noise I was very familiar with by that point – which alerted me to the plight of the burning bomber that night. Rather, it was the stuttering of its engine, a staccato thunder that broke the silence of our bedroom. As soon as we heard the noise, we leapt out of bed and made for the window. What we saw made all three of us shriek. A cascade of fire was coming from the bomber, which by then was flying very low. It lit up the inky night sky and left a blazing trail as it skimmed the top of the trees. The engines were struggling to stay alive – they would stutter and then almost die before suddenly bursting back into life, then they would stutter again. As the plane lumbered forward, barely clearing the treetops, two huge flames came from its crippled engines. It was running on empty, much of its return fuel having leaked away over the North Sea.

War, to us kids, had so much excitement to it. We didn't realize that within that doomed bomber were six young men who only had seconds of life left. They were not much more than boys themselves. Their spirits must have soared as they reached the English coast and left the dark expanse of the sea behind them – they were so very nearly home. Only twelve miles separated them from their base and safety, but they had been losing height for many miles and suddenly the engines died completely. At that moment all hope was lost. The bomber dropped like a stone into the trees and a great ball of flame shot up. Seconds of eerie silence followed before a series of loud explosions rocked the night air. I remember feeling the shock waves at the open window. Then silence came again. Only the continuing flames told of the horror which had unfolded before our eyes.

5

Tom

A World at War

ONE COLD DAY I WAS PLAYING INSIDE when I heard a strange sound. It was a bit like the bell on my dad's bike, but much deeper and louder. It was going on and on and I thought it was never going to end.

'What's happening, Mummy?' I asked. 'What's that noise, where's it coming from?

'They're ringing the church bells, my bonny boy,' she said. 'Dearie me, of course you've never heard the bells ring!'

I must have looked a bit puzzled because Mum laughed and tweaked my nose kindly.

'They stopped the bells for the war but we've just won a great victory over Jerry so we can ring them again just for this one day.' She gathered us three kids into a big hug. 'At last we've got something to celebrate!'

It was November 1942 and finally the German advance had been halted at El Alamein, the sleepy little railway junction only sixty miles west of Cairo. El Alamein was a last stand for the beleaguered British in North Africa and we had won. The 8th Army – the 'Desert Rats' – were on the offensive and driving the Germans back. It was a battle we had to win and it changed the course of the war.

We kids couldn't have understood the impact of this news at the time, but I remember jumping stiffly up and down with my sisters, our arms clasped tightly to our sides just like East African Maasai warriors we had seen pictures of in the paper. Mum was so excited she was beside herself. I'd never seen her like that before.

'We're only supposed to ring the bells if Jerry invades,' she shrieked. 'They'll ring them from Land's End to John o'Groats to tell everyone that Jerry's coming. But Mr Churchill has given special permission to ring them today . . . isn't that kind of him? Goodness me, this is all so exciting!' She picked me up, gave me another big squeeze and twirled me round and round. I fell over when she put me down, I was so giddy.

'We're going to win this war, we're going to win this war,' she shouted with an animation I'd never seen in her before. Three months after this, in February 1943, came the crushing defeat for Germany at Stalingrad. Maybe the Russians rang their bells too.

War to us kids seemed part of the natural order of things. It was all we had ever known and I couldn't imagine a world without it. The grown-ups never talked of anything else, and we incessantly played games about it, my favourite being one that involved running around with our arms stuck straight out like wings. We'd pretend we were aeroplanes, zooming along bending this way and that for all we were worth, and we'd sing a little ditty about the Nazi leaders. I'm certain it was the first song I ever learned and I still remember the lyrics to this day. It ran:

> Hitler has only got one ball,
> Goering has two but very small,
> Himmler has very similar,
> But poor old Goebbels has no balls at all.

It was sung to the tune of the 'Colonel Bogey March' and was very naughty considering we were so young. I took care not to blare it out in front of Mum, even though the adults didn't seem to mind much when we poked fun at Jerry.

My early years were very happy and danger always seemed to take second place to family life and love. Whatever ailment or anxiety we suffered, my parents would somehow manage to make it all right. I remember finding visits to the smithy quite upsetting at first. Dad would go every so often to get the carthorses shod and I would tag along, but I simply could not get my head around the way the smithy lifted the red-hot horseshoes from the glowing forge and tried them for size against the keratin of the horses' hooves. I swear they used to sizzle with the heat of contact. The smithy would go to the anvil and hammer the shoe to the size of the hoof, and all the while the horse just stood there as though it were enjoying the whole experience. Maybe the horse knew how good it would feel when it trotted off later in its fine new shoes. Horses are, after all, smart animals with very good memories. But I didn't know how the horse could cope with the smithy hammering long nails through the shoes and into the hoof. Each hoof would take fifteen minutes to fit, an excruciatingly long time when you're small and tense.

'Don't do that, you'll hurt him,' I shouted out when I saw it happening for the first time. I was quite unable to comprehend how nails could be driven into a living thing without causing damage and pain.

One day, shortly after this, an exciting addition was made to our little family home. Running into our tiny cottage, we three children came across a metre-high solid wooden rocking horse. It was gigantic, as big as a rocking horse can be, but somehow room was found for it in the hallway. I had never felt such elation before, and little as I was – especially in relation to the lanky Monica – I would still manage to fight my way up into the saddle for my share of the fun. Cecil and Elsie knew that I had been upset by the smithy and they knew just how to make up for it. While war raged in the world outside, tranquillity reigned within our little house. If only it could have lasted.

6

Jean

A Difficult Homecoming

I ARRIVED BACK in the village of East Kilbride, twelve miles to the south of Glasgow, in November 1939. I worried that I might be the cause of gossip. My pregnancy wasn't a secret and I felt sure that word would have got round when the official from the Foundling Hospital made his visit. Even if my parents had managed to keep the affair quiet, how could people not see that I'd changed and that there was now a part of me missing? But there was no gossip and no scandal. Everyone understood that the capital was in peril and that I'd come home to be with my family and escape the bombs. I was the same sensible girl they had always known me to be.

I had not been looking forward to that first evening at home with my parents. Even though they knew about the baby, we had not talked about it properly and I was afraid of what they might say. It was one of the most difficult conversations of my life, much worse than opening up to

55

Muriel. Although they had been spared the ignominy of a daughter displaying her fallen status in the village, they spoke of the shame and humiliation they had felt, and my father revealed that he had questioned whether his position as an elder in the Kirk was tenable given the circumstances.

My mother, who I'd thought would be the most judgemental, was actually rather supportive. She put her arms around me when I started crying and rocked us both until the whole sorry story had come out. There were tears in her own eyes by the time I'd finished. I know that she always nursed a private sadness and a sense of guilt at what had become of her grandchild, and from that day she never failed to send a present at Christmas and on his birthday. We didn't realize until many years later that these were never passed on, in keeping with the Hospital's belief that it would be unsettling for the child concerned and unfair for those whose families had written them off.

My father's reaction was another matter and the most upsetting. He physically recoiled when I admitted that Raymond and I had been sleeping together, and I realized then that he would never be the same with me again. It was as if I'd personally betrayed him. I felt chastened by his stern words and it took several weeks before he could even stand being in the same room as me.

I knew that I must find work – something to keep my mind busy – so I returned almost at once to my old job at the law firm. I don't know whether there was a vacancy, or whether my former boyfriend Hugo, who was the owner's son after all, had pulled some strings. It didn't really matter; I was just pleased the firm would have me back after learning about my pregnancy from the Hospital representative, Mr Long.

It only took a few days for Hugo to come calling. As I exited the office one evening, a figure stepped out of the darkness of a doorway and grasped my arm.

'You won't get away from me that easy.'

'Hugo, you frightened me,' I scolded, walking on.

'Aw, now come on, Jeannie. I know why you've come back. London's obviously no contest with Glasgow if I'm not there!' he said with a big grin. 'Let's go for a drink and you can fill me in on all the loose living you city folk get up to.'

I rolled my eyes but I couldn't say no. Hugo was a friend and I wanted to catch up on his news as much as he wanted to catch up on mine. One thing led to another and I eventually agreed to resume our relationship. I hadn't heard from Raymond in months and I thought he must have forgotten all about me. It was an upsetting time and I felt very lonely at home, so when Hugo said that he had missed me and wanted me back in his life, I found that I couldn't refuse. We enjoyed spending time together – it was all so easy and fun and just what I needed after those agonizing months in London.

What I didn't know at the time was that Raymond had

been planning to return to England. He had been unhappy in Africa for months but felt trapped because he didn't want to let me down – he was so keen to prove himself, and so worried about living up to the line he had spun about a future in that continent, that he felt to come back would be an admission of failure. Then the war came to his rescue: he could return with honour and fight for his country with no questions asked. However, when he received news (probably from one of his nosy sisters) that I was dating Hugo again, Raymond was crushed – he'd always been possessive of me and must have been consumed by jealousy and hurt that his old rival was back in the frame. When he reported for officer training with the Highland Light Infantry at Maryhill Barracks near Glasgow, he made no effort to contact me.

Six months later, unbeknown to me, he was back in Africa, seconded to the Royal West African Frontier Force as a subaltern. Hugo, meanwhile, faced the prospect of conscription. With the evacuation of the British Expeditionary Force from Dunkirk, there seemed little prospect of striking back at Germany on land for years to come. Only in the air could a young man expect to see meaningful action. For this reason, Hugo decided that he would apply to the RAF, where, as a clever young man with an aptitude for maths, he was trained up as a navigator.

But first he asked me to marry him. Hugo said that he

was to be posted away for God knew how long and he wasn't prepared to risk losing me again. I had been expecting this development and had decided to say yes. I thought the world of him, and although my love for him wasn't as strong or as deep as it had been for Raymond, I had no doubts that Hugo would make a good husband. I also had to consider the fact that I was well into my twenties by now. Raymond had given up on me as far as I could see, and if I wanted a family, I had to act as there was no time to lose.

There were a few hurdles to my happiness, though. Since I wasn't prepared to write off my son, my marriage would have to be on the condition that Hugo would accept the fact of the baby and promise to help me retrieve him. There was a good chance that if I was married and could provide a stable home, the Foundling Hospital would consider returning its charge, but what if Hugo couldn't handle this and ended the relationship? I shouldn't have worried so much. When I finally worked up the courage to ask him, Hugo – as kind-spirited and light-hearted as ever – put his arms around me and hugged me close. He said that he had been expecting me to ask this of him and was prepared to look after the bairn as if it was his own.

Hugo and I found it difficult to spend any time together after we were married as he was stationed away, and having fallen pregnant, I had to stay on in my family home. I spent much of the time worrying about the terrible losses that Bomber Command were starting to sustain in their growing aerial assault on Germany. Whenever he was home on leave, Hugo, true to form, would make light of the risks he faced and insist that he had every intention of seeing out the war. I knew that the aircrew were suffering the highest fatalities of all the armed forces so this didn't comfort me very much.

In December 1940 I gave birth to a girl, Maida. Hugo managed to get a few days off and it was a joyous time for us. He cradled our daughter and told me that we were all going to have a happy life after the war – 'You, me, this little one and her big brother'. It melted my heart to hear him say this and I loved him even more for his generosity of spirit.

Hugo was flying deadly bombing missions over Germany – which meant he was away a lot. He found the missions exhausting and frightening. The scariest part for him was not when they were over enemy territory – the adrenaline was flowing too fast by then – but as they droned their lonely way over the North Sea. With no coordinates to lock on to, and an endless stretch of inky water below, the only thing to do was think about what lay ahead.

As they approached the enemy coastline, Hugo knew that their radar presence would already have betrayed them. Some German private would have given their co-ordinates to nearby fighter units as well as ground-based anti-aircraft guns. Then he would wait with mounting anxiety for the much faster enemy fighters to come into view. On night raids, he dreaded the large numbers of searchlights that criss-crossed the sky and the thought that, sooner or later, one would home in on him. A pilot caught in a beam would struggle to escape before yet more searchlights locked on and he was 'coned'. At that point, there was almost no hope of escape as all the anti-aircraft guns would concentrate their fire on the highlighted plane. Death was almost certain. It was mercifully quick if it happened before the bomber discharged its payload, then the heavens would ignite with fire and flame.

By the spring of 1943, Hugo was still some way off the thirty-two tours that would see him grounded. He would let slip occasional hints of the strain and tiredness he felt when he came home on leave and I feared more than ever for his safety. With reason. One morning, shortly after he had returned to base, a telegram messenger, accompanied by a policeman, walked up the gravel path and handed an envelope to my mother. I knew instinctively what that telegram held and ran inside to be with my daughter. I hugged her close and wept bitterly.

'Missing in Action' was the term they used. It usually meant death but I knew there was also the slim possibility of a bailout or crash landing. For weeks I tried to cling to the idea that Hugo might have been taken prisoner or even sheltered by friendly locals, but as weeks turned into months and still there was no word – no concrete proof that Hugo had been killed – I decided I couldn't bear to wait any longer. I had to know for certain whether or not he was dead. So I caught the train to the air base where Hugo had been stationed and befriended a young officer in a nearby pub. After I explained my situation, he told me, strictly off the record, what the Air Ministry would not: that Hugo had come down over the sea; that his plane had been tracked by our own radar over the Channel and intercepted by enemy aircraft. All radar contact at that point had been lost.

It had been a strange mission, not the kind Hugo was used to, and how I wished he hadn't been tasked with it. Rather than taking the fight to the Germans, Hugo had been asked to drop supplies for the partisans deep in occupied France. Only a single plane was required. Hugo had a reputation as an exceedingly gifted navigator, and it may be that his skills were judged to be of the right sort to find the clearing in the forest. He must have felt so lonely up there without a fighter escort or a host of accompanying bombers, flying deeper and deeper into enemy-occupied territory.

That Hugo, whose life had promised so much, appeared to have met such a terrifying end gave me nightmares for years. I used to picture the moment when the shattering burst of fire ripped into his tail, the efforts he must have made to stop the plane spiralling out of control into the inky sea below, the black tunnel of his terror as he realized nothing could be done. Did he think about me just before the impact? Even my parents, who had once been so critical of Hugo, came to miss his sunny nature and devil-may-care outlook. It was a shattering end to my hopes of settling down with Hugo after the war and recovering my baby. I'd lost my husband and best friend, and the chance to get my little boy back and have the happy little family I'd always dreamed about. It had all slipped away with that telegram.

7

Tom

Paradise Lost

FOUR YEARS INTO MY HAPPY CHILDHOOD a terrible event occurred. Cecil died, suddenly and mysteriously. He was relatively young and the strongest man I had ever known. Later in life I learned that the cause was a duodenal ulcer, something people rarely die of today, but back then medicine and surgical techniques were much less sophisticated and perforation followed by internal bleeding could prove fatal. It was a catastrophic loss and I cried endlessly.

When Janet also vanished from the house, the damage to our little family unit seemed irreparable. It was then that I came to understand for the first time that Janet and I were not the same as Monica. We were not Cecil and Elsie's own children; we were foundlings who belonged to some faraway Hospital. I had always known that I had a different surname, but I'd never attached any importance to that. To find out that I didn't belong in that little cottage

– and that I'd have to leave myself the following year – was so overwhelming I could barely comprehend it all.

When Janet went, something in the house went with her. It wasn't as if she was boisterous, like me; in fact, she was quite the reverse – she always held back from the most adventurous dares which Monica and I would plunge into without a thought. But she was a good, sweet girl – always smiling, always cheerful – and we missed her terribly. One evening, late, after I'd been put to bed, I woke up and, seeing a light on downstairs, padded down to find Mum hugging a cushion to her breast in one of the old armchairs by the hearth. She was crying. I asked what was upsetting her but she wouldn't say, so I clambered onto her lap and watched as the glow from the embers of the fire died. To lose a husband and a child in the space of a few months must have been devastating, and I'm sure she dreaded the thought of losing me too.

Mum told me that I would be able to see and play with Janet when I joined her at the Hospital, but I was still unable to get my head around the fact that I wouldn't ever see my dad again. I went regularly with Mum to visit the cemetery. It was a long way from the gates to the grave and we'd walk along this little pathway which was flanked on both sides by low-lying privet hedges. The smell was very distinctive, almost slightly sweet. I rarely come across it now, but when I do, the scent of those tiny white flowers carries me back through the years to that sad time and the lovely, lovely father who disappeared from my life. It made a lasting impression on me to think that a person who had meant so much lay beneath the sinking mound close to my feet.

Before too long, another man moved into the void that Dad had left. He was a Scot and everyone called him Jock. While good to Elsie, he lacked my dad's warmth and love of children. I could tell that he resented me, the foundling whom he regarded as a cuckoo in the nest. He knew about Janet and used to taunt me about the Hospital when Mum wasn't around.

'One down and one to go. We'll soon be seeing the back of you,' he'd say with a sneer. I don't know what I did to upset him. He got along all right with Monica but he seemed to resent me – and before long I grew to hate him. He made me feel like I didn't belong in the home I regarded as my own, the only home I'd ever known. I used to tell Mum about it in the beginning, but this would almost always trigger an argument and I knew I'd be in for it later when he got me on his own.

'You're a little snitch,' he'd hiss, 'the sooner you're gone the better!' He used to get angry enough to pull his belt off and apply it to me viciously, and I'd soon feel scared every time Mum left the house. On one horrible day the buckle struck me and hurt so much that I became petrified of him striking me again. When Elsie saw the red marks from the buckle she flew into a fury and started laying into him.

'What have you done? Who the hell do you think you are?'

Jock fuelled her anger even more. 'What's the little bastard doing here anyway?' he shouted. 'It's hard enough looking after your own without forking out for someone else's.'

'That's not your problem. He was here before you came, and if you don't like it you can bugger off. You do this again and you're out.' Elsie stomped off slamming the door.

Even bad-tempered Jock would back down when Elsie was in full flood. He was wiry and strong, but he wasn't anywhere near as tall as Mum and I reckon she could have handled herself if he'd got violent. I bet Jock thought so too. Why Mum continued with the relationship I could never understand, but they did marry in the end, and I suspect my eventual departure from the scene may have helped.

It was a very unsettling time for us. Almost all the joy I had once known seemed to have vanished.

Mum's kindness made life bearable, but we were all so sad. It was as if there was a dark cloud hanging over the house. Monica missed Janet a lot and we would often talk about her and the games we used to play together. She was more protective than before once Jock arrived on the scene, and started to tell me off if I was being too noisy and kiss my bruises to make them better. She even tried to make me promise not to leave like Janet had, but of course I couldn't promise that, even though I wanted to. Oh how I wanted to.

One day, just a month short of my fifth birthday, Mum came home and said she'd bought me something very special. It was a little white sailor suit with a navy scarf and cuffs fastened with brass buttons. There was even a nautical cap. I rushed upstairs to try it all on, as proud as punch, thinking about all the sea battles I could re-create now I had a naval costume. But when Mum told me the suit was my leaving outfit, the one I'd wear for the journey to the Hospital, and that I must be a brave boy like all the men fighting for our country, it took the shine off everything. I felt wretched and burst into tears.

Monica cried with me.

'It was bad enough with Janet going, and now we have to lose Tommy too. It's not fair, it's just not fair,' she wailed between sobs, and then stomped out of the room.

Mum bent down and put her arm around my shoulders and tried to console me by saying that I would soon see my sister Janet again, and that she would look out for me in the Hospital. Her efforts didn't do much good, though. Jock stood by with a look of quiet satisfaction written all over his face. He wasn't the least bit affected by my distress and I swear he even smirked when Mum drew me into a big hug. In later life, I used to muse about whether he would have been so hard on me if he'd known that I was a child from his homeland, a Scot like himself. Maybe it would have taken the edge off his anger.

A week later I was dressed in the sailor suit and standing on the back step of our house. It was a lovely spring day, bright and sunny with a breeze that made the cherry blossom dance overhead. Mum took my hand, picked up my little case and together we walked down to the town square where a coach was waiting. There were a few Saffron Walden mothers already on the coach with their children, all looking decidedly glum. The journey to the Hospital took about an hour as we kept stopping en route to pick up more mothers and children. It wasn't a happy expedition. There was very little talking and one mother at least was already sniffling into her hanky.

As the coach drove along it made me think about all the children who had been evacuated over the last few years, torn from their homes in the cities and sent into the countryside where they would be safe from the bombing raids. I'd seen pictures of them in the newspaper, standing in their hundreds at railway stations with grim faces and sad little brown labels round their necks. They too had endured tearful goodbyes with their mothers, unsure when they would meet them – or indeed their fathers, who were mostly away at the front – again, so I knew that we foundling children weren't alone in our misery, but this didn't make it any easier.

After what seemed like a long time, the coach climbed a very steep hill, at the top of which I caught a glimpse of the magnificent pile that was to be my home. I was awestruck. It was the biggest building I'd ever seen, and even from a distance it looked sparkly and new. As it happened, it was then only nine years old. We passed through two large wrought-iron gates, behind which lay an expanse of manicured sports fields with giant cedar trees dotted here and there. A metal fence, two metres high, reached out from the gates around the perimeter enclosing everything, and there were two small cottages either side of the gates, also pristine with neat lawns and newly laid flower beds at the front, which I later learned belonged to the groundsmen. There were finer houses at the rear of the Hospital for the teaching staff.

We drove slowly down a long driveway flanked on both sides by stone columns, almost like miniature Egyptian obelisks, each one with a lamp on top. At the end stood the Hospital church, its impressive steeple glinting in the sunshine. We passed by this into a quadrangle to be faced by another building, also with four grand columns. I didn't know it then, but I would spend very little time in this area as it represented an inner sanctum and no foundling was ever allowed to set foot in it except with special permission or under escort. Finally, the coach pulled up in front of another imposing building topped with another, smaller steeple and we all got out.

Gazing up at the pristine architecture towering over and surrounding us on all sides, I felt very small. It all seemed so perfectly ordered and tidy. Our mothers were impressed too and one even murmured that it was like arriving at Buckingham Palace. In pride of place, in front of the inner sanctum, was a statue of the founder, Thomas Coram. Although I didn't know that this grand old man in his quaint clothes sitting in his chair was our benefactor, I instantly felt drawn to him. He looked benevolent, rather like a kindly old grandfather, which is something I'd always wanted.

Lined up on the gravelled area were two rows of women in old-fashioned nurses' uniforms: starched aprons, flowing cloaks and little white hats. At the time they almost looked like soldiers on parade, but we quickly learned they were the staff from the infants' quarters, where I and the other new admissions would spend our first year before joining the school proper.

Clutching our mothers' hands, we were led through the columns and into a great hall with a squeaky parquet floor and oak-panelled walls. I looked up at the high, decorated ceiling and my mouth fell open in wonder. On one wall there was a picture of the grand old man who had been hewn from stone outside. Later we learned that the giant portrait of the founder had been painted by his friend and fellow governor, William Hogarth. In one hand, he held a rolled-up scroll which represented the royal charter he had

obtained from King George II in 1739 to establish a
'Hospital for the maintenance and education of exposed
and deserted young children'. A globe lay at his feet to
make reference to the fact that he was a seafarer by occupa-
tion, one who traded with the flourishing New England
colonies on the other side of the Atlantic. No one looking
at that seventy-year-old countenance could doubt for a
moment that he was a kind man. His cheeks were ruddy,
doubtless from those many ocean crossings, and his wavy,
shoulder-length white hair was luxuriant and flowing. His
aspect was one of deep compassion and I felt somehow a
little eased by knowing that he would be watching over us.
We would hear many stories about him over the years,
including how he'd despaired to see so many infants lying
in the streets of Georgian London, abandoned by unmarried
mothers who felt they had no other option. Often they
would leave their offspring in a rich person's doorway with
a short note attached saying, 'Look after my little one
because the Lord has forsaken me and I cannot.' I'm sure
the great man would have been mightily proud to see how
his charity had developed from the plucking of those first
babies out of the poisonous gutters to this splendid and
modern Hospital.

Some of the newly arrived foster mothers drew their
little ones' attention to the magnificence of the place, others
stood in silence, seemingly at a loss. Elsie held my hand,
squeezing it every so often to reassure me. My thoughts

were on Janet, but there were no other children anywhere to be seen. I came to realize that boys and girls were segregated after the first year, and many days would pass before I caught a glimpse of her.

All of a sudden one of the nurses gave a loud clap and this drowned out any hushed chatter.

'Silence, please,' she said, before giving a short speech about the strong Christian ethos of the Hospital and the importance of obeying the rules. If we did what we were told and respected those in charge, we would get on well at the school, she said. There seemed to be a hint of threat in her words and I thought to myself: *What if we don't obey the rules? What happens then?*

At the end of this talk, the moment I had been dreading finally arrived: our mothers were invited to take their leave and return to the coach. All the children burst into tears, and most of the mothers did too. Elsie clasped me in a tight hug, smothering me in kisses and imploring me to be a good boy.

'Do everything the nice ladies ask,' she told me. 'Say your prayers at night and God will look after you.' Tears were running down her face by then. 'You'll always be my boy and I shall think of you every day.'

The sound of sobbing echoed round the hall as distraught children clutched at their mothers. 'Don't go, Mummy!' screamed one. 'I want to go home,' pleaded another.

Then one of the nurses, a severe-looking one, clapped

her hands loudly. 'It's time, ladies,' she shouted at the top of her voice. 'Back to the coach!'

Within a minute, all the mothers were gone. A more sorrowful group of confused, unhappy infants it is hard to imagine. Some turned around – first this way, and then that – some sank to the floor in utter defeat, many made a headlong dash to the door through which their mothers had exited, only to have their way blocked.

The coach was no less a scene of desolation. For five years the mothers had loved and cared for their little charges, and now they had been forced to give them up, just as their birth mothers had done. Their pain was every bit as heart-rending. I'm told even the driver was not immune to the pathos about him. As he listened to the sobs from behind him, he drew a hand across his eyes and wiped away his own tears. Then he put the coach into gear and pulled away.

8

Tom

Crocodile Fashion

W HEN ORDER HAD FINALLY BEEN RESTORED to the bereft new arrivals, we were lined up in a column of fifteen pairs.

'Hold hands, children, boys with girls,' one of the nurses barked, 'and let's have quiet as we go.' I put my hand into that of the girl beside me and she clutched it tightly.

'Off we go. Follow me to your new home,' said the same loud nurse. I think she was the one in charge, although maybe it was just her loud voice that made her seem so. We were told not to talk and to pay careful attention to what was being explained to us. I quickly grasped that meandering, running and walking alone were not permitted – difficult demands for small kids. From then on, a silent two-by-two march would be the order of the day.

The journey to the infants' quarters was a salutary one. We passed along seemingly endless corridors and around dizzying numbers of corners on a route that seemed to go on forever. I felt certain that if I ever found myself separated from the others I would never be able to find my way back, which was a truly frightening thought. The main challenge was that the whole place had been built with an amazing symmetry so that every corridor seemed the same length and every corner turned at the same angle. There seemed to be no distinguishing features anywhere, and it would take me two years to be able to navigate my way around with any confidence.

The gap between this place and the little cottage I had left behind seemed an unbridgeable one. Given a chance, I would have returned in a second, even with Jock there, but I knew enough to be sure that this was never going to be possible. My mother had gone and wasn't coming back. I was surrounded by people, but they were strangers, and I felt utterly alone. For my entire life I have remembered the events of that frightening day with the utmost clarity. I felt numbed by the enormity of the experience.

When we eventually reached our destination, one of the nurses told us to put down our cases, which we'd been holding for a very long time by then, in the corner of the room. We paused, slightly dumbstruck by what was going on. With an outstretched arm, she pointed towards the corner.

'Come on, children, quick about it. We haven't got all day.'

I had only a few items in my case – a toothbrush, a round tin of toothpaste, a single change of clothes and, the bulkiest thing of all, a fluffy white rabbit that I used to take to bed with me at night. I had a sense I wasn't going to see my suitcase again, and I didn't want to leave my rabbit behind, but I did what I was told and let go. One of the girls fumbled with her case, trying to open the catch on top, which was proving difficult.

'Stop that,' a nurse said, going over to her. 'Just put it with all the others.' The girl later told me that she had been trying to get out her own toy, a caramel teddy bear with a green jacket, before putting her case down. She wept about the bear and talked a lot about how much she missed him during those first few months.

The head nurse led us into a changing room with wooden benches. They were numbered, and below each hook were neatly folded identical sets of clothes.

'Now, children,' she said briskly, clapping her hands. 'You must all take off your clothes and put on these new ones.' Silence followed as we tried to process the command.

'But mine are new!' I finally blurted out, feeling that I'd isolated the most important word in the instruction.

'Never mind that, just do as you're told. Get these on,' she said sharply.

But I was hugely proud of my new sailor suit and didn't want to take it off. 'I don't want your clothes. I want mine! Mummy bought them specially. And I want my rabbit too.

My daddy gave it to me and it's in my case. Please can I have it?'

The nurse glared at me with a look of shocked outrage before she responded. 'You won't be needing them any more. We have our own things here. Now, are you going to argue with me, little boy?' It was clear she wasn't used to being challenged. All the other children had frozen, awaiting the outcome of the stand-off. None moved to take their clothes off.

'I want them back,' I said crossly, teeth gritted and both hands on my hips.

Another nurse entered the fray. 'What's your name?'

'Tommy,' I replied. I could tell that this nurse, too, was irritated and was marking me down as a troublemaker, but she could also see that I wasn't easily going to take no for an answer.

'Look, Tommy,' she said in a softer tone, perhaps concluding that a more conciliatory approach might do the trick. 'All the children have some fluffy thing or other. Lots of them are dirty – not up to our standards – and you could catch germs from them. They're unhygienic. And you'll keep mislaying them and expect us to send out search parties to find them. There will even be scraps when one of you wants to borrow another's toy. Be sensible, Tommy. It just isn't practical.'

But I wasn't having any of it. 'I still want my rabbit back,' I persisted.

'I'm sorry, I just can't give it to you. It's against the rules.'

It was clear that their normal orderly induction was under threat and the loud nurse cast an exasperated glance in the direction of the one who'd been trying to reason with me. She moved to grab me and put an end to what she saw as a disruptive show of defiance by forcibly removing my clothes herself. A third nurse approached, sensing that this might not end well.

'What's all the fuss, little man? We only want you to try on your nice school uniform. We're not taking your own clothes. You'll get them back.'

'You promise?' I was desperate at this point to believe what she said. All my peers were standing watching me and I felt so alone in my struggle.

'We promise.'

But I never did see my sailor suit or rabbit again. They were my last tangible links to home, a world that was lost to me.

Taking their cue from me, all the children changed into their new clothes, except that they weren't actually new – they were clearly the previous year's hand-me-downs, a fact I found particularly galling. It then remained only to fit us out with shoes. A large box full of used pairs was carried in and the nurses set about matching shoe to child. With all of us now sitting in a circle with our shoes on and laces trailing, the loud nurse who had locked horns with me walked into the centre of the ring.

'Pay attention, children,' she said in her overbearing voice. 'I'm going to show you all how to tie your laces up, and I'm only going to show you once.'

With that, she slowly performed a contortionist trick with a lace. Anxiety gripped me. My mind was still on my sailor suit and my rabbit and I feared I'd missed the essential part of the technique. What if the other children had got it? I risked utter humiliation at the hands of the nurse I'd so vexed minutes before, and would then be a marked boy, with all the unpleasant consequences that were sure to follow from that. Miraculously, though, my tormentor announced that she would break her golden rule and show us all one more time. I felt a huge sense of relief, and this time round I determined to give it a level of concentration beyond anything I had managed in my life before. It was the beginning of a long journey of avoiding humiliation and staying equal to, or ahead of, the pack that would obsess me for the rest of my life.

After a bowl of thin broth, it was bath time – an experience which proved particularly traumatic. Not only was the water scalding to the point that I could barely lower myself into the tub, but I suffered the indignity of having to share it with a girl at the other end whom I didn't know. After this, we were expected to brush our teeth in the washroom where fifteen wash-hand basins stood back to back with fifteen others. Each of us had been assigned our own basin and a demonstration was given as to the correct method. We each opened the small round tins given to us by the nurses and found a hard pink slab wrapped in cellophane. With the brush moistened, we brought the bristles across the slab and all was ready. Then, with a clap of the hands (hand-clapping seemed to be de rigueur), we were instructed to begin and told not to stop until we had been given leave to do so.

I learned in the weeks ahead that the more dedicated I appeared to the task in hand, the sooner it would be over. I tried to do everything exactly as we had been shown, and as quickly and efficiently as possible. While performing our daily routines, we'd fix our gaze on the supervising matron, desperately seeking to catch her eye and gain the sought-after nod to stop.

As bedtime approached on that first day, I began to see that my life would be one of habit, order and ritual. We marched off to the dormitory – in crocodile fashion as instructed – and then waited as we were each assigned a bed. There were thirty of them, all in one room, fifteen on one side and fifteen on the other, with a large oak table running down the middle. It was so different from the cosy little room I had shared with Monica the night before, and I worried that I wouldn't be able to fall asleep somewhere so open and public.

Before getting into bed, we were instructed to kneel and put our hands together in prayer. Here, as elsewhere, a parquet wood floor had been laid, and my knees felt its hardness. After a short prayer, a piano struck up in the semi-darkness and two nurses began singing a hymn. They invited us to join in, and although it took a few weeks, we all learned the five verses word for word. It became a favourite in the infants' quarters, though the poignancy of the lyrics would be lost on me for many years to come. Verse one began:

> There's a Friend for little children
> Above the bright blue sky,
> A Friend who never changes,
> Whose love will never die;
> Our earthly friends may fail us,
> And change with changing years,
> This Friend is always worthy
> Of that dear Name he bears.

I like to think that there was a certain maternal tenderness in this choice of hymn and that the nurses used it as a way to articulate their own sadness at the circumstances, which did not permit them to mother us as perhaps they might have wished.

To an outside observer it would have looked like a touching end to the day – thirty kneeling children in little nightdresses clasping tiny hands in prayer. To me, not yet five years of age, it had been a truly terrifying one that I would never forget. Many years later, at the Charter Day Dinner which the charity holds annually at their London headquarters, I asked my fellow foundlings what they had felt that first day. Every single one of them remembered it with a similar clarity. What died that day was love. It died for all of us. From the moment our foster mothers handed us over, all the love that a child can expect to receive from its parents was cut off. However much the nurses tried to ease that bleakest of transitions, they could never replace the warmth of our mothers. If I think back to that first night, when I lay on my cold iron bedstead between starched white sheets, I can still hear the sobs of those lost, lonely children rising from all around me. I remember wiping away my own tears, thinking of Cecil and Elsie and all their closeness and love. It would soon be a distant memory.

9

Tom

The Infants' Quarters

AFTER A FITFUL NIGHT, we were woken at six-thirty a.m. and told to pull our sheets and blankets to the end of the bed for airing. It was still quite dark and I rubbed the sleep from my eyes, wishing it was all a bad dream. We filed out behind the nurse to the washroom, where the same teeth-cleaning ritual was performed as the night before. Then it was off to breakfast, where I struggled to eat the bowl of stodgy porridge placed before me. The misery of the previous day and the worry about what was to come had played havoc with my tummy, but it seemed that all food must be eaten, no matter how we were feeling or how unappetizing we felt the dish to be. This was followed by prayers, and then we were all marched to the lavatories where we would remain until a solid had been achieved. This part of our daily routine was designed to induce a regular bowel action so that the nurses would not be plagued, as the day proceeded, with children asking to be excused. No one could leave the loo until the product of his or her labours had been inspected. If we felt we had succeeded, we could invite a nurse over to review the evidence. If she felt that it was insufficient, we would be obliged to resume until something more substantial had been achieved. Never could the evidence be destroyed. Only a nurse could authorize a flushing.

After this, it was reward time. For those who had achieved an early flush, there was the inestimable treat of being first to the toy cupboard to get the tricycle or another prize toy of our choice. Needless to say, this moment was one of high excitement and acted as a major incentive to get the bowels moving. I can still picture that large cupboard, just under the big staircase leading to the dormitories. It was an Aladdin's Cave and always put a smile on our faces.

One of the hardest things to get used to was the lack of freedom. In the open fields behind our cottage in Saffron Walden, I and my sisters had been free to roam and play virtually unsupervised. Monica, as the eldest, might have considered herself to be in charge, but she was only three years older than me. In those days neither parents nor children worried about bad things happening. It was an idyllic existence, especially in spring and summer when the fields were covered in dandelions and daisies and we'd play all day until the flowers closed up and the evening chill took over. From the very moment I entered into the care of the Hospital, however, all that freedom vanished. We were watched day and night and needed permission to do everything. There were so many rules and regulations. You could only go out to play when you were given leave to do so, and we all had to play together, all thirty of us. A beady eye ensured that no one wandered off to do their own thing. It is true that the surroundings were beautiful and the playing fields enormous, but like everything else in the Hospital, they were orderly and manicured – not like the wild countryside I was used to. There was no way to find a bit of quiet somewhere on my own, and it took me a long time to adjust to the constant jabber of voices and the occasional shrieks of children at play.

There was one inmate above all others who I did want to seek out, though – my sister Janet. I was constantly on the lookout for her at playtime, in the dining hall, at chapel, round every corner. After a few weeks I finally saw her from a distance in the playground one morning. The infants had a special little area all to themselves. The older children couldn't enter this space and we were forbidden from leaving. Putting on my most plaintive look, I approached the nurse whom I had come to regard as the kindest.

'Nurse, please, can I speak to my sister over there? I haven't seen her for ages. Can I say hello to her?'

The nurse looked at me with what seemed like real tenderness in her eyes.

'Point her out to me, Tommy. I'm not supposed to allow this, but I'll see what I can do.'

I pointed to Janet, a giddy sort of hope rising in my chest. 'She's the one over there with wavy black hair,' I explained.

'You stay here,' she said before scurrying over to where Janet was and leading her back to me.

Janet had grown a bit in the year since I'd last seen her. She smiled that sweet smile of hers and I smiled back. Always shy, it took me a moment to give her a little kiss.

'Do you know when we're going home?' I blurted out.

'Shhhh,' said Janet, putting her finger to her mouth. She looked fearfully at the nearest nurse who was a few yards away. Luckily she didn't appear to have heard.

'Oh, Tommy, I'm so glad you're here,' she said in a hushed whisper. 'I so hate this place.'

I saw real misery in her eyes and felt so sorry for her that I leaned in to give her another little kiss and took her hand in mine. I hated to see her so upset. She was such a tiny thing and it must have been even harder for her than it was for me, especially now that she had left the infants' quarters for the upper school.

I asked her again, 'Do you know when we'll be going home? I asked Nurse, but she wouldn't say. Do you know?'

'We won't,' replied Janet with a sorrowful look in her dark brown eyes. 'They're keeping us here till we're fifteen.'

'Fifteen,' I exploded. 'Fifteen! We'll be like grown-ups. That's not fair.'

It was such a shock that I started to cry, which started Janet off too, and then the nurse saw our distress and came to lead Janet away. I felt wretched. It had been over a year since she'd left home and I wouldn't see her again until I joined the upper school – and even then strict segregation of the sexes meant that we wouldn't spend any time together.

At times it felt like we were in a prison, albeit a well-tended and modern one. The large wrought-iron gates we'd passed through in the coach were kept permanently shut. I realized that the perimeter fence was too high and awkward for even a seasoned climber like me to scale; for years none of us ever passed beyond it. That warm, lovely world beyond the Foundling Hospital receded gradually into a blur. Eventually it was lost to us altogether. There was a quaint little town at the bottom of the steep hill on which the Hospital stood which had a lot of history and charm, much like Saffron Walden, but we would not get to see that for years either. There would be no visits to the shops with Elsie, no stopping to buy gingerbread men wrapped in brown paper, no meeting with friendly neighbours who would pat me on the head and sometimes give me a sixpence. In time we would all accept that this was how it was, but at first there was a strong sense of abandonment.

Mum had told me that I would be coming home with

Janet during the school holidays, but that turned out not to be so. I don't know whether she had said that to cheer me up – a little white lie, so to speak – but the fact was that at the start of the war the Hospital had suspended the practice of letting children return to their homes for holidays. By the time I joined the school, four and a half years had already passed, but no one knew then that peace was just eighteen months away. I started to worry that I would never see my mother again.

With so much fear and upset, it was no wonder that nights were difficult. Some of the children cried every night and there was a lot of bedwetting and nail-biting. The nurses wouldn't wait until the morning to change the stiff white cotton sheets because of the smells and their bustling would often wake up the whole dormitory. Those who suffered in this way, and that included me, had a rubber sheet to help protect the mattress, which might have been sensible, but was also deeply humiliating. I had bad dreams and used to cry out in my sleep, and some children used to sleepwalk. I'd never come across this before and found the spectacle quite frightening. I'm not sure whether they were prone to it or had developed the trait as a result of the Foundling Hospital experience, but I wouldn't be surprised if it was a response to the trauma of separation – an unconscious bid to escape the Hospital and find a way back to their families.

One or two of the nurses tried to be a bit motherly and

sometimes they might put their arms around your shoulders or rub your back if you were upset. You never once got a kiss out of them, though. Maybe it was against the rules, in case it looked like some children were receiving preferential treatment. The nurses had their favourites, of course. These tended to be the submissive ones who did exactly as they were told and never rocked the boat. Sadly that wasn't me. I tried at the beginning to be anonymous, to keep my head down so I didn't get picked on, but I was inquisitive by nature and asked too many questions for my own good. At home if I'd remonstrated with Mum over this or that, she had listened patiently until I'd had my say before deciding whether to give ground or hold firm. In the Hospital there were few, if any, concessions made to the disruptive ones. Thirty youngsters arguing the toss would, I have to admit, have wreaked havoc, and so we had to learn to keep our mouths zipped. This was a real challenge for me, but I was scared of the consequences if I didn't. Although kind for the most part, the nurses were not above administering punishments when they thought they were called for, and the threat of a swift slap on the wrist or ears meant that I was afraid to push my luck too far.

The nurses always seemed rather old to us though I don't suppose they were much older than our mothers. I later learned that many of them had been in service but had lost their jobs after the First World War because the landed gentry couldn't afford them any more. This would certainly help to explain their fixation with cleanliness, which was exhibited during one of the most degrading experiences that happened a few days into that first week: We were instructed to stand by the ends of our beds with our underpants held up and turned inside out. The nurse then walked down the line, inspecting each pair very carefully. A quarter-way along, she stopped, screwed up her face and pinched her nose. Then she took a step backwards and let out a loud 'Aghh . . .' followed by a long, drawn-out, 'Dis-gus-ting!' She demanded that the miscreant step forward to the centre of the dormitory and reveal to everyone the 'horrifying' exhibit of his dirty pants. As she moved down the line, more were subjected to the same treatment. It was a humiliating, even cruel procedure, but it did have the effect of causing us to take greater care over our toileting efforts.

There were many strange things to get used to in my new life – and they often involved standing in a line. I remember the nail-clipping in particular. We would all have to stand with our hands out in front of us while the nurse went along the line doing the business, but she didn't do it like Mum; she was faster and didn't pay the same attention. When we squawked, she'd say, 'Don't be silly, it isn't that bad.' Of course, when you're operating something like a production line and you want to get to the end of it as quickly as you can, you're not going to take the same care.

While not as painful, the process of cutting our hair was something else we didn't look forward to as the scissors were almost always blunt and used to pull at the roots. It was a no-nonsense business and the boys would all end up with scruffy crew cuts. The girls got more upset than we did because, being girls, they were used to different, shall we say more flattering, styles. But in their case, as in ours, homogeny had to rule. Funnily enough there had been a period before my arrival when an ex-hairdresser had been in the employ of the Hospital – and a much better job had been done – but she had left and so it was back to the anything goes approach.

We must have looked so alike, so institutionalized, with our matching hair and uniforms. We boys were dressed like smart little soldiers in chocolate-brown trousers and scarlet waistcoats with brass buttons and a high white collar. On Sundays a bow tie was added and a sideways military-style cap. It was an altogether splendid outfit, quite the equal of those in any of the country's elite private schools such as Eton or Harrow. The girls were not so lucky. They had to wear long dark dresses with a white pinafore attached which made them look like domestic servants. Little white maids' hats were perched on top of their heads to complete the look. I suppose these were rather fitting as historically boys had joined the forces and the girls had gone into service. Times were changing, though, and many of the girls felt that their attire was dated, particularly as they got older and wanted to look more fashionable.

The fact that we didn't see much of the older children during that first year was probably just as well as we were miserable enough getting used to all the rules and regulations and life without our mothers. At five years old, I don't think I could have coped with the rough and tumble that would come from mixing with the boys in the main school. We began to realize what we were in for quite early on, though. Each day a nurse would take us on a three-quarter-mile walk around the Hospital grounds, and sometimes on these occasions we would catch sight of the children who had moved up to the school proper. They would shout down catcalls from the upstairs dormitory windows, and instead of doing the sensible thing and ignoring them, we would respond in kind. They must have hated our infant taunts. We probably should have thought more carefully before provoking them by calling out as we passed, but at the time we felt safe with our escorts and immune from retaliation.

'Don't worry,' they would shout back. 'We'll get you back. You'll be ours before you know it. Just a little while, just you wait!'

10

Tom

A Trip to America

We quickly settled into the rhythm of the infants' school and each day would pass in much the same way as the previous one, with strict times for meals, chores, exercise, play, church and school. Every activity was regimented and every minute accounted for by those in charge.

I enjoyed my time in class, perhaps because it was one of the only ways to unleash some creativity. I learned to read from a book which featured a dog called Rover, who proved a fine substitute for the ferrets, which I missed. I'd even pretend he was following me around sometimes; an imaginary friend, if you will. There were two infant classes of fifteen and we definitely had the nicest room. It was decorated with a whole series of farmyard animal tiles and we'd often pick one at random and make the appropriate noise. We were also lucky in getting Miss Pickles. She was a tiny woman with a neatly cropped dark bob and a singsong voice – very much like Edith Piaf, as I later discovered.

From time to time she'd excuse herself for a short period and would often select me to come forward and keep the class amused with a story. It was a signal honour and I loved standing there, giving free reign to my imagination. My tales usually involved animals, and wherever possible I would introduce something scary, like wolves or tigers. But it was a little daunting. What if my inspiration failed one day and I dried up with stage fright? There were some pauses occasionally, but I used to wrestle hard in my mind and the storyline would always emerge in one form or another.

The infants in the other class had Miss Brown. She was older and stouter than Miss Pickles and much stricter, and she used to shout a lot. Any pupil whom she judged to be slow or naughty would be made to stand in the corner of the classroom for fifteen minutes with a 'dunce's hat' atop their head. The hat was brightly coloured and rose to a sharp point; it looked ridiculous and certainly did its job of humiliating the 'useless' child. I'm so glad I never had to wear it or stare at the wall with my back to the class.

We spent a tremendous amount of time outdoors – either playing games or taking part in organised sports. I really enjoyed rounders and would run hell for leather to get round the four corners before the fielder returned with my ball. Sports were one of the only ways to distinguish ourselves later – to do well and get ahead – and they meant a lot to us. We were split into four houses: Coram, Handel, Hogarth and Dickens, which helped to develop a strong sense of competition that would remain with us throughout our years at the Hospital and beyond, but this competitiveness also meant there were often fights among the boys that the nurses had to intervene in constantly.

But we had quiet moments too, making daisy chains or inspecting the latest flowers to emerge from the fertile soil – tiny white snowdrops, then clusters of primroses, then the bright yellow daffodils that spoke of the coming sunshine. Bluebells were my favourite and they would always reach their peak around my birthday in May. We didn't receive any cards or presents and nothing was said to us about birthdays, so they went by unmarked, year after year. That first summer seemed very long without some sort of celebration, since Mum had always made a big thing of them. When I got to the upper school I became aware of the calendar, so at least I knew when I was a year older, but it took the bluebells to lift my spirits on the day itself, and as an adult I always seek them out in the beautiful Devon woodlands where I live. It's one of my great pleasures in life to walk along the mossy ground, carpeted with purple, and breathe in that delicate sweet smell.

Music was our one true love at the Hospital. We were always singing, and we learned folk songs as well as sea shanties and hymns. Later on many of the children were taught to read sheet music and could play their instruments magnificently. I used to sit in church and think what a great privilege it was to listen to the beautiful voices of the choristers. In my early years, church attendance was twice every weekday and three times on Sunday. We didn't complain. The church was an impressive building with its ornate columns, stained-glass windows and mighty bell tower, and listening to the choir, accompanied by the magnificent sound of Handel's own organ (the one he had used every year to perform his *Messiah*), gave us all a little peace. Sometimes the emotion could be quite overwhelming.

My first Hospital Christmas was certainly enlivened by the many church services. We came out singing carols and they'd echo down the corridors and in the classrooms. No cards or presents were exchanged, but the Hospital authorities did encourage us to celebrate. We made multicoloured paper chains, which we hung in the dormitories, and the hall was decorated with beautifully ornate Chinese lanterns and a tremendously large Christmas tree – a gift from one of the wealthy benefactors. There was certainly a jauntier atmosphere than normal, and within the limitations of my new life, I did enjoy the season.

It was a bitterly cold December in 1944. Snow lay everywhere but there was no let up in our daily exercise and play regime, and we would all huddle together, desperately trying to keep warm. We were never cold in the dormitories, though, as the Hospital had a very sophisticated heating system. I once went to the boiler house to see it in action, and marvelled at all the pipes, which were enormous and spotlessly clean. Everything was underground, though there was a sizeable building on top for access, perhaps so that if it were to explode, the blast would be contained and go upwards rather than sideways and bring down adjacent buildings. How Mr Bishop, the man in charge, understood all its workings, I'll never know. He was tiny, but he commanded a lot of respect because he knew what to do with all the complicated dials and levers. Always smartly dressed – dapper, you might say – he never once wore overalls or a boiler suit. Those were for his underlings.

The stodgy food also helped us to keep warm, but while we were luckier than some to get meat every day in wartime, we didn't feel very grateful at the time. There was always a thick yellow fat covering it so you'd have to chew and chew before finally giving up and swallowing the gristle whole. You had to eat everything: mutton, white beans, rice in clumps, semolina – it was all loathsome, and there was almost no fruit, which is one reason we would go 'scrumping' in later years; we all knew that stealing was wrong but the lure of those juicy apples from the orchards was too hard to resist. The worst thing about mealtimes was that you had to get it all down, every last bit. I absolutely hated tapioca and most of my classmates felt the same. It looked like frogspawn and made me want to retch, but down the hatch it had to go, like everything else.

Carrots were a struggle for everyone too. Raw ones I didn't mind, even liked, but the Hospital used to boil them up until they were grey and mushy. The nurses tried to make swallowing them a little easier by telling us that carrots were the reason our pilots were shooting down so many German planes in the dark. By gorging on them, so the story went, the pilots were absorbing a special eye-enhancing compound which improved their night vision and allowed them to pick out the fighter planes. Jerry hadn't cottoned on to this yet and thought we had a top-secret weapon. Although I half believed the daft tale at the time, it didn't work. No matter how terrifying I found the dark or how much I wanted to emulate our boys in the skies, I simply hated the soggy carrots too much and nothing and nobody could make me want to eat them.

Mealtimes were regimented like everything else. The whole school would march into the hall, sit down together, and then say grace: 'For what we are about to receive may the Lord make us truly thankful.' We weren't allowed to talk to each other or share food, which made it monotonous and not very pleasant, and to add to that the hall seemed very dark because the walls, like so many in the Hospital, were oak-panelled and the windows very high up. The girls were screened from the boys by moveable wooden shutters – and we infants ate on the girls' side of the dining hall. I suppose the authorities considered us gender neutral at that young age, but we boys felt it was a terrible dig to be regarded as girls – to have to eat with them and bathe with them. There was some relief on special occasions, such as Christmas and Easter, when the shutters separating us could be opened, and that made for a jollier atmosphere. The boys would sneak curious glances at the girls, and I was always, always on the lookout for Janet.

There was a steady stream of bombers passing overhead that winter. Although I didn't know it at the time, the war, which had been raging for five years now, was nearing its end. Avenging armies were closing in on the Reich from east and west, and our bombers were pounding Germany from one end to the other.

Everybody had their own gas mask, including staff. They didn't look quite so grotesque and comical on the larger heads of the adults, but on us they looked truly ridiculous. When the nurses weren't paying attention, we used to put them on and run around trying to spook each other. We'd become so familiar with the drone of the aircraft overhead by now that we could tell if they were home-grown or enemy engines. In the event of enemy planes, we would head for the air-raid shelters, but if there was insufficient warning, we'd just grab our gas masks and dive under our beds. During one memorable incident, one of the German flyers parachuted out of his shot-up plane and the house-masters rushed out to capture him. I don't know what they would have done if he'd pointed his Luger pistol at them; probably run off back to the dormitories and cowered under the iron bedsteads with us.

If they were our own planes going off to bomb Germany,

we shouted and cheered from the dormitory windows, 'Give it to Jerry, give it to him!' The planes were so heavy with bombs that it would take them some time to gain height, and they would only have reached a few hundred feet above ground level by the time they reached us even though the American airbase was about four miles away. You could feel the building shake. We used to push up the sash windows of the upstairs dormitories and lean out as far as we could. One of the girls almost fell out once and we only saved her by grabbing at her dress. There would be a long line of children – seniors as well as juniors – leaning out along the entire length of the Hospital and cheering their heads off and sometimes the housemasters would join us. The pilots could see us all quite clearly and would wave back. Often there were a hundred or more planes and they used to make a point of flying in one great long line, one after the other. It was the most remarkable sight – and we absolutely loved it. I spoke to one of the pilots years later and learned that they could have gained the extra height if they had really tried. 'But what the heck!' he said. 'We knew how much you kids loved it. You were there at the windows every time.' The planes would return home just a few hours later, fewer in number and many beaten up.

They were our heroes, those American boys, especially after they invited us over to 'America' for a party. It seemed big-hearted Uncle Sam was determined to give us an experience we would never forget. Between operations, their trucks collected us – fifty at a time – and drove us over to the base, and there, lined up, wing tip to wing tip, were rows of the death-delivering machines which, along with their British counterparts, were pulverizing the cities of the Reich. They allowed us to climb along the gunners' turrets and into the cockpit, which was thrilling beyond anything my friends and I had ever dreamed of. Then, after some Disney movies and party games, we were treated to an array of goodies that were scarce in wartime Britain and forbidden by the Hospital – including chocolate!

Years passed before I realized that I had not actually visited America, and I would argue fiercely with any of my peers who disputed the fact. I hadn't realized there was the small matter of an ocean to cross first. I returned to the airbase much later, long after it had been abandoned at war's end, and there, rusting away on the runways, were the relics of a tiny part of that great American and British air armada that had visited such terrible destruction on the enemy. As I stood there it seemed a tragic paradox that the young Americans had been making such an effort to lift our spirits while the broken bodies of numberless other children caught up in the raids they had carried out lay a few hundred miles across the sea. An American secretary of defence summed up the dilemma during the Vietnam War when he questioned, 'How much evil must we do in order to achieve good?'

11

Jean

So Near and Yet So Far

AFTER HUGO DIED, I started writing regularly to my friend Doris whose baby had also been taken into care by the Foundling Hospital. The threat of bombing, which had driven me home from the capital, had indeed become a reality, but not quite to the apocalyptic levels predicted in 1939. And as the war ground on and the Luftwaffe were driven from our skies, my thoughts returned to London. Doris invited me for a weekend visit and made a startling suggestion.

'Look, Jean, I know you miss your little one as much as I do mine, so I've had a thought. Why don't we try and get work at the Foundling Hospital? There's nothing to stop us. We could apply for anything going – carers, cleaners or kitchen staff. What do you think?'

My heart leapt at the idea, but I had Maida to think of and I didn't see how we could possibly pull it off.

'I don't know, Doris. It sounds awfully risky. I'd have

to leave Maida with my parents for a while and what if we're discovered? There would be consequences.'

'Nonsense. What consequences?' She took my hand. 'Chances are they won't cotton on, and if they do, so what? They'd sack us! It's no crime to want to be near your child.'

She was right, I reasoned to myself. We could apply and see what happened. A glimpse of Derek would be wonderful.

'Go on,' pressed Doris. 'Say yes. We can really do this!'

'All right,' I said, not feeling Doris's bravado but half happy to allow myself to be persuaded. I thought how brilliant it would be if the plan did come off, and my mind quickly turned to practicalities.

'There are going to be lots of little children running around. I'd like to think that I'll know which one my Derek is, but what if I don't? He's a little boy now and he'll have a new name. If we can get some form of work or other, it will be pretty basic stuff and we won't have access to the files.'

'Ah, but Jean, love, the Hospital might be able to change their names but they can't change their birth dates now, can they? They all have birthdays. We send cards and presents every year, and so must the other mothers. So we'll be able to see who gets our gifts and this will tell us what we need to know.'

It seemed to make sense, though in keeping with my

more cautious nature I remained a bit sceptical. Of course, we had no way of knowing whether our cards were passed on, but I went along with the plan because the reward of seeing my child was too tempting not to try.

On our first visit to the Hospital, a reconnaissance mission that weekend, we were both dumbstruck by the size of the building and grounds.

'It's awesome!' exclaimed Doris.

'Absolutely beautiful,' I agreed.

We didn't dare enter through the gates, but we were filled with excitement when we saw a group of children running around in the distance. They looked so healthy and so real. I couldn't quite believe that one of them might even be my Derek.

Doris asked a friend to go to the Hospital headquarters in Bloomsbury and pick up application forms for us, and as soon as she returned, we realized the whole project was impossible. They required a wealth of background information before they would allow anyone to come and work for them: not just names and dates of previous employers, but information about our families and even our medical history. Later, when I thought about it, I realized they would almost certainly have had a list of all their children's mothers to check job applications against, as they would have been alert to enterprises of the kind that Doris and I had in mind. For a time Doris wondered whether she could come up with enough false information to deceive the Hospital as to her true identity, but I knew it was hopeless. My little Derek seemed further away than ever.

12

Tom

Lords of the Dorms

ALL TOO SOON THE DAY THAT we had all been dreading arrived. It was autumn 1945, we were six years old, and it was time to join the main school. The girls had less to worry about as they would be moving to the half of the school reserved for them, where the regime was strict and monotonous but generally benign, whereas for me, I knew, this upheaval would be almost as traumatic as entering the Hospital a year ago. I was headed for the other half and would spend the next few years at the mercy of the older boys and their punishing, violent games.

Although all we boys were worried, I had more reason than the others. Over the last six months there had been a few incidents when I had shown myself to be something of a ringleader, and I felt sure that I had already been marked down as someone to be dealt with. The first episode had happened on a winter's day on our walk to chapel when we passed a snowman. The seniors had obviously spent a long time building it and it was massive. I looked at the boy in front and we shared wicked grins as we broke rank and started laying into it with gusto. Following suit, all the others broke rank too and shared in the demolition until it had been kicked to smithereens.

'Now you've had it. We'll get you for this!' screamed the older boys, who had appeared from around the corner and were running at us with rage in their eyes. 'You've really had it now. Just you wait!'

I laughed scornfully at them as we moved away under the protection of the nurse, but I got a shock a week or two later when my imagined anonymity was well and truly blown away on one of our morning walks.

'I know your name,' shouted a voice from one of the upstairs dormitory windows. A senior was looking down and pointing a finger straight at me. 'You're Humphreys. You're top of our list for special treatment when you come over – you'll see!'

I was shaken and instantly afraid. I didn't know how they had found out my name. They must have asked one of the staff since everyone in my year, the nurses included, called me Tommy. It was only in the upper school that you were known by your surname, or rather the surname that had been given to you by the Hospital, so the very sound of the name 'Humphreys' made me uneasy. It suggested a big tough boy, which I most certainly was not.

The threat of retaliation made me quake in my boots and I started to wish I hadn't led the charge against that snowman, but in truth I knew there were plenty of other reasons why that boy and others might want to make an example of me. I was always among the first to answer back, and I'd 'cheek' them, as they saw it, if one of them shouted something from their part of the school. I even made rude hand gestures when the nurses weren't looking. By now they almost certainly viewed me as someone who needed to be brought down a peg or two.

My fears increased a few weeks before we were due to leave the infants' quarters. We were walking two by two as usual one morning when we turned a corner and saw three boys beating up a much smaller one. Two bulky lads were holding the junior's arms while a third was laying into him with his fists. He wasn't aiming for the boy's head, since that would have left marks, but instead for his solar-plexus – that tender point just beneath the rib cage where maximum pain can be inflicted without it being obvious.

'Stop that, stop that!' the nurse shouted when she saw what was going on, making the boys scatter as they left the junior on the floor, badly winded and gasping for air. I was surprised to see how fast the nurse hitched up her skirt and ran after one of the larger boys, but he was faster still and got away.

'I want their names,' she said, returning to the poor junior who was splayed out on the ground. 'I want their names. Come on now, tell me.' He just shook his head and groaned something about not knowing them. Neither she nor we believed him. She knelt down and rubbed his back with a sigh. Breaking the code of silence was unthinkable. If he snitched on his attackers, they would be hauled up in front of the headmaster during the morning assembly and caned, and this would of course spell a much worse punishment for the nark later.

I dreaded the strict discipline of the housemasters almost as much as I did the brutality of the older boys. In the infants' quarters we were rarely exposed to any physical punishment. The nurses would occasionally lead us by the ear somewhere, or if we'd been especially naughty we might earn a sharp slap on the back of the hand or ear – but nothing that would leave a mark. In the upper school things were very different. A long bamboo cane was considered the answer to miscreant children and it was used quite liberally. The offence would be read out at morning assembly and followed by 'six of the best' – a phrase that would send chills down our spines ('best' meaning hardest). Exemplary punishments were always carried out in public by the headmaster, Mr White. He had a fearsome reputation but it was nothing compared with that of his predecessor, Mr Holgate. I met one of his victims a few years ago. He was eleven years older than me and had been struck repeatedly and so hard that three operations in later life were unable to correct the damage done to his hand.

As much as we disliked the group routine and lack of peace in the infants' quarters, at least it sheltered us from the harsher realities of the upper school. We always travelled under escort and as a unit, and we'd never been required to think for ourselves. Now, along with evading the malice of the older boys and the wrath of the masters, we would be expected to be self-sufficient. There would be no nurse to defend us or push us back into line if we strayed. Even the thought of navigating my way around the gargantuan school was frightening. I also knew that I'd miss the girls, and in particular, Martha. Having had two sisters as playmates I enjoyed girls' company, and Martha had in many ways become a substitute for Janet. She slept in the bed next to mine and we used to whisper a lot to each other after lights out.

'I'm going to miss you, Tommy,' she said on the last night. 'I don't know who they're going to put me next to, but it's going to be horrible.'

'Don't worry,' I replied. 'We'll be in different dorms, but at least we'll see each other in the classroom. Maybe even sit next to each other.'

I quickly realized, however, that this was a no-no. Boys sat next to boys at the front of the class where the teacher could keep a beady eye on them, and girls, considered less troublesome, sat further back. It was a strategy that worked in terms of our lessons, because we couldn't distract or tease the girls without turning 180 degrees, which meant we were forced to get on with our work, but we didn't play or eat with them any more either. They went to their half of the school and we went to ours. I always imagined that daily life was a lot easier for them than us. I'm sure they had a few bossy girls, but they can't have been as violent as the boys we had to put up with.

It had been my hope – the only thing that sweetened the pill of moving up – that I would see more of Janet, but I saw less of her than ever. We were in different years, so were never in the same class, and the girls had their own playground, quite separate from the boys'. I couldn't even blow her a kiss if I saw her from a distance as I had done in the infants' playground because the fear of being labelled a sissy by the other boys was far too great – this was a no-kissing world. The most I ever attempted was a sly little wave from a low angle when I thought no one was watching.

I tried to keep my head down and my mouth shut during the first few weeks in the upper school. The older boys treated us with disdain and we avoided eye contact with them as far as possible. Fortunately the boy who had marked my card earlier seemed to have either forgotten or found some other poor sap to pick on. I thought the transition was going as well as could be hoped until one day when I was passing a group of seniors along the corridor a hand shot out and clipped me round the head.

'Ow, what was that for?' I yelped without thinking.

The senior, by now a pace or two in front, stopped me dead in my tracks, in tandem with his hefty companion.

'Did I hear something, Entwistle? It almost sounded like a protest. Like a little squeak from a mouse perhaps, but still a protest.'

'I think you did, Grainger,' he replied, turning and fixing me with such a hostile glare that my heart missed a beat.

'Was there something you wanted to say to us?' asked the burly Grainger.

'No, nothing,' I said quickly, looking down at my feet.

'Right, well then, in that case we'll be off. There's just the little matter of your name and dormitory first, *boy*.' He dragged out the word boy as if making a point and took a notebook out of his top pocket. I mumbled my name, wishing the floor would swallow me up. What would he do with it? I thought for a moment about giving a false dorm, but he would find out the right one in the end – which would make things worse. My dorm monitor, the older boy who was in charge of policing us, would make sure I paid for my lip.

That was the last time I ever challenged an older boy. The thought of ending up as the choicest cut on the menu for that night's dormitory entertainment was terrifying, but nothing ever came of it. I can only suppose that he considered me too little to be worth bothering with. Older boys seldom beat up a younger one as they deemed such conflict beneath them; if they wanted to make an example of a little boy they'd select one of his peers to do the dirty work. I was six and still very small for such treatment. I judged the whole encounter to be a lucky escape and resolved to learn my place and never be rude to an older boy again.

Bedtime had been unpleasant in the infants – what with all the crying and bedwetting – but now it became grim to the point of terror. Each dorm had a monitor, an older boy who slept in the corner of the room and had sole control of the boys in his care after lights out, and we used to lie awake trembling and waiting to see what 'game' ours would dream up next.

The housemaster for our dorm had a flat at the far end of the corridor and round the corner, so he couldn't hear what went on, and 'skit keepers' would be posted at various points along the corridor to give warning if he decided on an unscheduled visit. When a subdued 'skit' was whispered from the corner nearest his flat, it would instantly be relayed to the second, third and sometimes fourth boy before reaching the dormitory. The housemaster would barely have a chance to walk a dozen paces before a mad scramble would be underway for everyone to get back into bed and turn the lights out. It was a virtually foolproof early warning system and never once, in my experience, did it fail.

The reason such elaborate precautions were necessary was that the monitors had a vicious sense of fun. They

THE LAST FOUNDLING

would delight in thinking of new ways to hurt or humiliate us younger boys – from ordering us to have fistfights to seeing how long we could stand in stress positions to holding us out of the window until we begged for mercy. We would all cower beneath our sheets, hoping against hope that it would not be our turn that night. There was no arguing or standing up to the monitor: his power was absolute.

Blanket-tossing up to the eleven-foot-high ceiling was a favourite in my dorm. A group of boys would be summoned to hold the edges of a blanket and a boy would be thrown into the middle. Then he would be tossed up and down, banging each time against the ceiling. Suddenly the blanket would be yanked away and the boy would crash to the parquet floor. My reflexes were quick and I could usually get my feet down in time to save myself but others weren't so lucky. Ours were young bones and breaks were rare, but the bruises were often severe and the pain would last for days. 'Omertà' was total: no one ever reported the true circumstances of an injury – it would always be put down to some plausible accident like slipping on the stairs or trapping one's hand in the door.

The monitors loved 'games' that caused the maximum amount of pain but left no signs of violence, and many 'good' ideas were passed along to the less imaginative monitors in other dormitories. One wheeze that spread quickly involved taking a light bulb out of its socket and ordering

115

a boy to touch the metal contactor inside, so that he would electrocute himself. This was cruel enough, but then someone with a particularly sick mind thought it would be even more hilarious to form a line of boys, each one holding the hand of the next, so that when the first made contact with the metal tip in the socket, the whole line would be convulsed. Each boy would be ordered to lick the palm of his hand to improve the conductivity through the line.

We endured years of this kind of torture – until we were old enough not to need a monitor any more. The only respite was for a few weeks one year when a prank in my dormitory went badly wrong. A boy was trussed to a chair and lowered out of the window which was twenty feet from the ground below. At about the point he began his descent, the longed-for 'skit' was heard. Such was the panic to get back into bed that the boy tied to the chair was quite forgotten and those holding on to the rope just released their grip. He crashed to the ground and sustained serious injuries. How the whole issue was resolved none of us ever did get to find out, but the boy never made a reappearance after his period of hospitalization. There were whispers of a broken back. The Hospital had an amazing capacity to keep things under wraps. Police, local authorities and government agencies were all in awe of its ancient charity status and powerful establishment governors, and few had the courage to ask questions or make waves.

It was a lonely, unforgiving existence but we all had to put up with it. There was no one to turn to for relief and no one to stand up for us. Even though we were all going through the same testing ordeals, we never banded together and there was no camaraderie. We were too busy fighting our own individual battles to think about helping anyone else. Each night we'd all pull the covers over our heads, ingesting our own fetid, recycled breath and hoping to submerge ourselves in a black cocoon of safety that would last until morning. It was a small world under those covers, but it was the closest thing we had to being on our own; a private space where nothing could intrude, except perhaps, the ugly, bawled shout of the monitor.

13

Tom

A Watery Grave

IT BECAME VERY APPARENT TO ME as the months went by that the only way to survive in this climate of fear and retribution was to become feared oneself. There was a strict pecking order based on the many fights arranged by monitors. These would happen during the day but out of sight of the staff, usually in some corner of the grounds far away from the main school buildings. Each monitor would choose a champion from the dorm of boys he presided over and then there would be a tournament to establish who was top dog. Every single foundling knew his position as a fighter, and those who could not give a good account of themselves were miserable in the extreme, because everyone would pick on them; almost anyone was at liberty to terrorize them. I felt sorry for the weaker boys and decided not to join in with any bullying. Their existence must have been an unbearable nightmare. I cannot think that their psyche could ever have recovered in later life.

Although I was quite mean in a scrap and had no difficulty looking after myself, I was no good at punching. I
could never land the killer blow and was rarely chosen to
champion the dorm in any sort of fist fight. My strength
was wrestling. I could always incapacitate an opponent by
wrestling him to the ground and holding him there until
he cried out 'I surrender' for everyone to hear. It was less
violent than fist fighting but still a great way of establishing
my dominance over the other boys, and this ability to
wrestle well used to stand me in good stead when, as older
children, we'd play 'British Bulldog' in the gym. It was one
of my favourite games, and an opportunity to assert myself.
We were all so fiercely competitive that the play could get
quite nasty, and there were a few cracked bones and many
black eyes and bloody noses over the years – fortunately a
bloody nose was the worst I suffered.

The Hospital seemed to encourage this tough, competitive streak within us, perhaps thinking that the stronger
and more resilient we became, the better we would be able
to survive in the outside world. We didn't often see it like
this at the time. And of all the scary physical ordeals we
were forced to endure, learning to swim was definitely the
worst. It was absolutely terrifying. As infants we weren't
allowed to go near the pool, but in our first few days as
juniors we were propelled along the corridor in nothing
but our underpants, knowing that we were headed for the
water. It was highly unusual for a school, let alone one for

abandoned children, to have an indoor swimming pool and the teachers clearly thought we should be grateful for such a luxury, but as we lined up along the edge of the pool, cold fear gripped us all. I can still remember rubbing my arms, trying to make the goose pimples go away before I got into the water.

After piling into the shallow end, we were quickly obliged to duck our entire bodies, including heads, under the waterline. Eyes screwed up tightly and nose pinched, we did this over and over – bobbing up and down – until the teacher thought he had adequately proved that total immersion would not harm us.

Then an older boy was called upon to demonstrate breaststroke and we were invited to copy what we had seen. Armbands were out of the question. After much flapping and spluttering, we were mercilessly driven into deeper water. Battling to stay afloat and eager not to consume the entire contents of the pool, we kicked with all our might until we reached the side. All, that is, except for one unfortunate backslider. He began to sink in the deepest part of the pool, taking in huge mouthfuls of water and grasping desperately at a long rescue pole that had been extended to him. He finally clutched the pole, only to be pushed back down before the teacher drew on his end and hauled the hapless lad to the surface, coughing and spluttering and streaming tears, but thankfully still in one piece.

Unsurprisingly, it wasn't long before we all became

competent swimmers. By the end of that year we looked forward to our lessons, and by the time we left the school we were as comfortable in the water as on dry land. My fear of drowning never quite went away, though, thanks to a bout of water-wrestling that nearly went wrong for me. The teacher had left us to practise front crawl but we decided to fool around for a bit till he got back. The object of the game was to try our hardest to keep our opponent under the water as long as we physically could. I must have been about eleven, and the boy I was grappling with had me in a vice-like grip. He was doing his damnedest to prevent me coming up for air, and it suddenly occurred to me that if I didn't get out of the headlock pretty much now, I was not going to make it. Luckily I managed to knee him in the stomach and squirm free, but I felt rather shaky afterwards.

As a consequence of the Hospital's unforgiving regime, we foundlings became formidable competitors in swimming galas. I won my county colours at thirteen, and particularly enjoyed relays, as the team was almost always made up of foundling boys and we used to thrash our opponents. I remember taunting a losing group after a particularly savage race once and claiming they were 'lesser mortals'. We were the water babies that the Hospital had always dreamed of – true sons of our naval founder Thomas Coram.

The Hospital was undoubtedly better at physical education than academic. There were no exams, except to establish the class pecking order, and the teachers didn't seem to have any sense of a curriculum. No one was expected to go on to university, and there was always a greater focus on good behaviour than achievement. This was especially true when the male teachers flooded back to the Hospital after the war. They were determined to firm up discipline and for a couple of years there were more canings than ever before. Mr Benton, a wiry air-force man, was a fiend with his yard-long bamboo cane. He kept it on top of his bookcase and would sometimes startle us by reaching for it while we all had our heads down concentrating on work. He'd caress its long length before bending and swishing it through the air with relish – you could tell he was itching to try it out on someone. Mostly he would just use it as a cruel way to intimidate us, but occasionally he would whip it furiously on the desk of a boy who had got his sums wrong – and then on his behind if he still couldn't get the answer right. Maths was my least favourite subject and I lived in fear of that cane. I was quite good at mental arithmetic, but if there was any sort of written problem to be solved, I would clam up with worry. It was hopeless, almost like a curtain coming down on my brain. I hated being punished for my perceived slowness, but with no mother or father to complain to the school on my behalf, there was little I could do. We had no voice, so I endured Mr Benton and his reign of terror in silence.

14

Tom

Home for Christmas

CHRISTMAS IN 1945 WAS an extremely happy period for me. Following six years of war and another six months to let the dust settle, the Hospital finally decided that it was time to resume fostering in the school holidays. I hadn't seen Elsie in eighteen months, but some children hadn't seen their parents since 1939, and we were all giddy with excitement. My joy was all the greater because I had been dreading Christmas in the upper school. The infant nurses had done their best to give us a happy time the year before, but without their singing and cheer, the whole occasion was going to be dismal – and I feared the bullies would concoct some form of sick merriment to pass the time.

On the morning of our departure, a fleet of coaches arrived and one by one made their way across the gravel of the inner sanctum, slowly coming to a stop in the quadrangle which we were not usually allowed to enter. One coach was for Chertsey, another for Addlestone, and there were others for all the dormitory towns surrounding London, but of course the most exciting of all was the one for Saffron Walden. It must have been a logistical nightmare to make sure that each of the six hundred kids managed to get on the right coach, especially after years without any practice, but the teachers were so happy about it all, and wore the broadest of smiles – it was amazing to see the entire complement of staff waving us off, including the dour Scots housemaster Mr Homan. I'd never seen him smile, but there he was, grinning with the rest of them. Even the older boys who usually made a point of standing on their dignity wherever and whenever possible were hopping up and down in anticipation.

I looked around for Janet, apprehensive in case she wasn't there. When I finally saw her amongst a small group of girls queueing up for the Saffron Waldon bus, I was so happy that I immediately went over and took her hand. I didn't dare give her a kiss, much as I wanted to, because there were too many boys milling around who might have made something of it later, but I did squeeze her hand tightly and she gave me the sweetest of sweet smiles in return.

'Let's sit next to each other on the bus,' she said, climbing up the steps. 'You can have the window seat. I've got so much to tell you.'

And so began the best trip I have ever made on a coach – the complete opposite of the one I had endured a year and a half before. Everyone was bubbling and chattering nineteen to the dozen before we'd even passed through the school gates, at which point a loud cheer erupted – and one boy at the back shouted, 'Good riddance to bad rubbish.' I thought he was going to be told off by one of the two staff members accompanying us, but they just shrugged and smiled. It was wonderful to see the Hospital recede into the background. I was finally on my way home.

It was only a few days before Christmas and the landscape was very bleak: the fields were grey and barren and the trees, which had long ago lost their leaves, looked like they had been stencilled onto the murky sky. But I didn't care and nor did Janet. I didn't even mind that Jock would be there when we got home. It was enough to be together and to know that Elsie and Monica would be there waiting for us.

And indeed they were, along with a large group of mothers and children, in exactly the same spot we'd caught the coach from so many months before. I grabbed Janet's arm and pulled her up from her seat, along the aisle, down the steps and into Elsie's arms. She was a little rounder and had cut her hair, but she smelt the same – a lovely mix of lavender and vanilla with just a hint of Lux soap. I can't imagine how the children who had been separated from their foster parents for the entire six years of the war must have felt. They weren't allowed to display photos in the Hospital and I bet some of them had forgotten what their parents looked like. For the foster parents, the problem of recognition must have been greater still.

Returning to Alpha Place was even better than I had imagined. Monica was beside herself with happiness and even Jock was on his best behaviour and greeted us warmly. 'Good to see you, kids,' he said, ruffling Janet's hair. He seemed to have mellowed towards me and his belt didn't come off once during the whole break. Maybe I didn't wind him up as much. The Hospital had certainly taught us the value of being quiet and well behaved.

After the vastness of the Hospital, it seemed strange to be living somewhere so small. I remember thinking that Gulliver must have felt like this when he was cast adrift into Lilliput. But the cottage was home and full of people who loved me, which made it easy to settle back into life there. The Hospital was set in beautiful grounds and its facilities were second to none – we had so much in a material sense, but nothing in an emotional one. I knew times had been hard for Mum during the war, especially after Cecil died and she had to make her rations stretch to feed three hungry children, but I would have given anything to rejoin that little family for good. No splendid grounds or steeples or swimming pools could ever make up for missing out on life at home.

It was so bitterly cold that we spent most of the holiday indoors. Even trips to the shops assumed something of a magical quality. Mum would wrap us up in two jumpers, long scarves and woollen mittens before buttoning our coats right to the top and pushing us penguin-like through the door. We set off at something of a waddle, but it thrilled me to peer into the festive shop windows and admire the red and green paper chains, strings of tiny lights and garlands of silver-foiled tinsel. My favourite was the bakery, not for its decorations, although there was an impressive tree sprinkled with sugary snow in the corner, but for the rich cinnamon warmth that hit you as soon as you entered. Mum would always stop in to buy a farmhouse loaf on her way home, and I loved the freshly baked doughy smell. After those long months in the Hospital, I'd almost forgotten what it was like. I used to wish she'd be tempted by some of the fancier delights – a sticky gingerbread, buttery mince pies or one of the sumptuous Christmas cakes made with whole cherries, black treacle and plum brandy. The cakes were lined up along the counter, some with elaborate wintry scenes including iced snowmen and little houses dusted with icing sugar and fine gold glitter. Mum said they were all really expensive but she did buy one slice on Christmas Eve which she cut into five smaller pieces so we could all try a bit. It was heavenly.

I was a bit upset to be cooped up indoors when I had such fond memories of running around in the butter-cupped, rabbit-infested field behind our cottage, but I told myself that I'd only have to wait a few more months for the warmer weather of the Easter holidays. And fortunately, Mum hadn't given away the rocking horse after both Janet and I had left, though Monica told me that Jock had argued for it to go.

'It's a bloody monstrosity', he had shouted shortly after I'd gone to school. 'Come on, Elsie, can't you see, it's far too massive for this wee house. Why not sell it so we can have more leg room?'

But Mum wouldn't have it. She was looking forward to the day when her house was full of children again and the rocking horse would be as treasured as it deserved to be.

I wasted no time in climbing up and having a play. There had been a rocking horse in the infants' toy cupboard at the Hospital but it was much smaller and made of metal so your bum always got cold. It wasn't a patch on Mum's, which was solid wood and a yard high with stirrups, reins and a proper saddle – the lot. 'It's rubbish' I used to say dismissively about the one at the Hospital. 'You should see the one we've got at home.'

On Christmas Day we opened our presents. Mum had knit us all scarves and I remember feeling sad because I knew that I wouldn't be allowed to take mine back to the Hospital with me. After attending the morning service at the local church, Mum took us to the cemetery where Dad was buried. The raised mound of earth had long since settled and I found it odd to think I'd been away for so long. Then I started to worry about my impending return to the Hospital. How much longer did I have at home? Should I try to savour every minute by reminding myself that it wouldn't last, or should I try to forget the Hospital altogether for however long I had left?

Once the thought of my return to the Hospital had lodged in my mind, even a trip to see a pantomime in nearby Cambridge didn't raise my spirits for long, though it was the first time I'd seen anything like it. I loved the way the audience was invited by nods and winks to boo the baddies, and I found it exciting, though a little scary at times, like when the evil queen tried to poison the pretty princess, but I held Mum's hand at that point and took comfort that she was there to protect me.

I had tried to talk to Janet about our return to the Hospital a couple of times during the holiday, but she didn't want to and turned away if I brought the subject up. On the bus home, she had told me a little of the girls' side. I had been wrong to think that their world was altogether rosier than ours, although it did seem that their housemistresses were a bit kinder. They had their share of nasty bullies, but instead of using violence to intimidate and oppress, the girls would find verbal ways of humiliating each other. Janet said that some of the taunts were so appalling that the more unfortunate girls would cry for hours afterwards. And worst of all, there was no mother to put her arms round you and make the world go away for five minutes. I hated to think of anyone picking on my sweet little Janet. It made my blood boil.

Returning to the Hospital was such a grim prospect that I hit on an idea. *What if Janet and I were to go missing when it was time to leave?* The Hospital authorities would eventually stop looking for us and we could then pop out from our hiding place and remain at home forever. Mum wouldn't need to tell the governors that we'd turned up; she could just carry on looking after us as she always had done – and that would be that. But when I told Monica about my idea, she immediately pooh poohed it and said how stupid it all was. There would be such a hoo-ha when we disappeared that everyone in Saffron Walden would know.

'What do you think the neighbours are going to say when you two eventually do pop up? "Ah well, it was all a bit of fun. Let's not say anything to the authorities and then they can go on living like happy families." Grow up, Tommy!'

Monica was three years older than me and quite scornful whenever I didn't think my schemes through. 'And another thing,' she said. 'Where do you think you're going to get all your food until they give up looking for you? From me, I suppose. Do you think Mum wouldn't notice all the food going missing?'

'But we wouldn't eat that much,' I tried. 'We're small and can last for ages on a bit of bread and butter.' I knew as I said it that my plan was falling apart. Monica put both hands on her hips and pursed her lips angrily.

'And do you know what else, Tommy? They'd say Mum knew all about it from the beginning, that it was even her idea. She'd be in big trouble and it would all be your fault. If she was taken away, where would that leave me? Without a mum or a dad or my brother or sister, that's where. You're mad!'

So that was that. Janet and I got back on the coach and headed to the Hospital with the other foundlings. The journey was miserable and hardly a word was spoken. When we arrived, I barely had time to say goodbye to Janet before she was whisked off to the girls' side. I knew that I wouldn't get to speak to her again before the Easter break – and that was months away.

The return to dormitory life was painful beyond belief. One of the perks of being a monitor was a permanently full stomach and ours helped himself to all the Christmas goodies we'd brought back for the weeks ahead. Pieces of toffee, mint humbugs and my mum's melt-in-the-mouth shortbread all went under his mattress. That first night was the worst. Everyone drew their blankets over their heads, and though it was against the Hospital ethos to cry, I imagine every single boy sobbed himself to sleep. I know I did. Even the monitor, with his bed stuffed full of our cakes and sweets, seemed miserable and turned the lights out early. There were no 'games' that night.

15

Tom

Big Boys Don't Cry

Shortly after that amazing Christmas break, the seniors decided we were ready to take on some additional responsibilities. We'd been in the upper school for seven or eight months by that point and obviously they thought we'd settled well enough into the regime to be counted on to perform the duties of a lackey without protesting or running to one of the masters. Every older boy was assigned a junior – the lackey – who would attend to his every need. Since only a small number of boys were able to assume the much-coveted position of monitor, this was a consolation prize for the less fortunate: a personal servant to boss around as they pleased.

It was a thankless role and one that I had been dreading. Along with taking care of the older boy's chores and smuggling food out of the dining hall for him, the lackey was seen as a source of fun and was often toyed with in a mean way. I once saw an older boy leap onto the back of his lackey and demand a piggyback ride through the school's endless corridors. The poor lad was tiny and kept buckling under the load, but the older one wouldn't get off. He found the whole thing hilarious and only ceased when the housemaster came striding out of his room to see what the racket was all about.

Sometimes two seniors would decide it was fun to club together and mess with a junior. 'Go and fetch my towel,' one would demand. 'I want my shoes polished,' the other would say. If the boy made a move to fetch the towel, he would find himself blocked. 'What about my shoes? Are you disobeying me?' If he then focused his attention on the shoes, the first boy would wade in: 'But I gave you a direct order to get my towel.' They would both aim to look as menacing as possible so the lackey didn't know what to do or who to obey. These stand-offs were never resolved and the younger one would quake with fear, trying to compose himself as he waited for the inevitable punishment.

Part of the problem was that the boys were so bored. The school routine was unvarying and dull, and this aggressive posturing was a way to liven things up as well as assert a degree of control over the surroundings. The fact that I understand this behaviour now didn't help me then, though. I considered myself incredibly unlucky when I was assigned to Entwhistle, the same senior who had terrified me in the corridor a few months before. He evidently held a grudge and tried to make my life as difficult as possible. One of his favourite ways of humiliating me was to make me lick his shoe before polishing it. I always blew as hard as I could to try and get rid of some of the dust and dirt before applying my tongue.

'Get a move on, Humphreys,' he would admonish. 'Get licking! What's the matter with your spit today?' He'd laugh at my discomfort before handing me the cloth to get buffing. It was horrible; my mouth would get dry and sooty and later I would find all these little cuts on my tongue. They would be sore for days afterwards. I was only glad that there wasn't a single dog in the whole vast establishment, so the danger of Entwhistle stepping in dog poo before I began my work was non-existent. That didn't make me hate him any the less, though.

One of the key duties of a lackey was to smuggle a meaningful portion of his meal out of the dining hall to give to his senior. We were almost always so hungry that our stomachs used to growl during afternoon lessons. The masters must have known what was going on, but they never did anything about it. I suppose they were reluctant to undermine the seniors in case discipline became threatened. The school relied on the principles of obedience and conformity. It was a bit like the military: the younger boys obeyed the orders of the older ones and everyone ultimately obeyed the masters.

I found the whole idea of saving my food to give to someone else really difficult. Jock had often complained to

Elsie, 'He's eating us out of house and home,' and it was true, I did have a very healthy appetite, and hard as I'd been trying to feed Entwhistle, it really wasn't easy. One evening he demanded that I bring him one of my sausages, but we'd only been assigned two and I couldn't resist eating them. I knew I would be in for it and was feeling rather sorry for myself when, on the walk back from the dining room, I saw that the kitchen was empty. This was very unusual, but I didn't hesitate – here was my chance to redeem the situation. Like Jack Flash I was in there. I looked around but couldn't see any sausages, so, desperate to find a suitable substitute, I opened a pantry door. The delay was my undoing. Into the kitchen from the far side strode the cook. She caught me red-handed.

My offence was judged sufficiently grave to warrant a public caning. It would be the first and only time I was caned in front of everyone at morning assembly. I knew that it was important to see the business through without making a sound – it marked one out as a 'sissy' and had to be avoided at all costs. I'd never cried during a classroom caning, and I was confident that I would not cry during this one, but staying totally silent was another matter. Tradition stipulated that you took your punishment without so much as a wince, which was hard. I wondered whether I could manage this if the cane came down much harder than usual. If I cried out, the whole school would hear.

I was extremely nervous on the morning. The assembly was a sacred part of the Hospital routine, and all would gather in the great hall, the girls down one side and the boys down the other. Not even a hushed whisper was permitted. Suddenly the doors would be flung open and the teachers would file in. They would make their way onto the stage and stand in a line, leaving a space in the middle. That space would be filled by the headmaster – Mr White – who would make the most dramatic entrance of all, sweeping in just before the Hospital hymn was struck up on the grand piano. I always enjoyed singing and would belt out hymns with all the fervour my small lungs could muster, but that morning I was far too nervous and my voice was reduced to a mumble.

The last piece of theatre was the caning itself. I went up onto the stage and put my hand out in front of me. Mr White administered a hard whack but I didn't cry out or even bite my lip. I managed to get through all six strikes without a sound. So did my fellow miscreant. We both left the stage with our heads held high and our honour intact.

The throbbing pain in my hand had faded to a dull ache by the next day and then, within a week or so, to nothing at all, but I had been left with something much more significant – a sense of pride in my own stoicism and fortitude. The Hospital placed a high value on being tough. There was, after all, no one to pick us up if we fell and grazed a knee; there was no one to give us a cuddle and kiss us better if we were distressed or poorly; no one to turn to for comfort or relief. No comfort anywhere. Having nursed my own children through many minor scrapes and upsets since then, I really don't know how we foundlings managed to get through. But get through we did. I don't think I ever witnessed public crying in the upper school. We had to be hardy and learn to survive without showing any sign of physical or emotional distress. It was a testing challenge, but one we were all compelled to rise to.

16

Tom

From Pillar to Post

THE RESUMPTION OF HOLIDAYS with our foster parents had given us something to look forward to, but when Easter finally arrived I was in for a terrible shock, the worst I could possibly imagine. On the morning of departure I was lining up for the coach when the teacher told me that there had been a change of plan. I wouldn't be going to Saffron Walden any more but to a foster home in a small Surrey town called Chertsey. Nobody would tell me why. I was devastated as I looked over at Janet and realized she was boarding the Saffron Waldon coach. I couldn't believe the cruelty of the situation. How could the only mum I'd ever known not want me?

I convinced myself that Jock was the arch villain; that he had dug in his heels and wouldn't let Elsie take me back. For years I believed this, but the truth finally emerged after I had left the Hospital at fifteen. Mum had become pregnant with Jock's child. In fact, she had been several months gone when I had stayed with her at Christmas, which explains why I thought she'd put on weight. In that tiny cottage there simply wasn't room for us all; something had to give and that something was me – I was a boy and that made me the odd one out. The girls could squeeze into the second bedroom but a boy was another matter, and although it might not have been a problem initially, it would have become so with the passage of time. Perhaps Elsie felt it was kinder to make the break while I was young and could find another home with people who wanted a small child running around the place.

My new foster home in Chertsey was close to the river Thames. It was a terraced house with an outside loo, which meant freezing my socks off if I needed to go at night. I suppose this was fairly standard at the time, but I was used to the Hospital's facilities now and saw it as a great incon-venience. Annabelle and Arthur, my new foster parents, were nice enough. He was a fireman and looked the bee's knees in his black tunic coat with shiny silver buttons, hard hat and heavy boots. While he looked extremely fit, Annabelle was the opposite: short, dumpy and rather homely. I didn't take too kindly when she announced, on the walk from the coach to their house, 'You've got to call us Mum and Dad. It won't sound right if you're calling us one thing and the boys are calling us another.'

By boys she meant their twins, Rodney and Roland,

who were two years my senior. I did as I was told, but it didn't seem right calling a couple of strangers Mum and Dad. For me there could only ever be one Mum, as there had only ever been one Dad. Even Jock had never made any pretence of replacing Cecil. And although both my parents had now gone from my life, I wasn't ready to let them go in my mind.

'Rodney, Roland, come over and meet Tommy,' Annabelle chirped when we arrived. 'You're to treat Tommy as one of the family from now on. Isn't it nice – you've got yourselves another playmate. How jolly!'

Rodney looked me up and down slowly. I could see that he wasn't impressed and I suspected he was more than happy with the playmate he already had. As for Roland, he didn't even bother to look at me. He seemed to be watching something out of the window. Neither said a word. It wasn't a promising start.

Later that day I heard the brothers talking in their bedroom.

'Where's he come from?' Rodney asked.

'Oh, I don't know. It's Mum's doing, isn't it? I don't think it's fair. Why should we share our bedroom with him?' Roland said. 'I'm not sharing my toys with him,' Rodney chipped in. 'Have you noticed he hasn't brought any of his own?'

There was no doubt that my new foster parents were very charitable, but I don't think they'd given enough thought to how I would fit in with their family. The twins had such a strong bond that there was no room for a third member, especially not one who was parachuted in without warning. Friction was inevitable and Annabelle found herself having to rebuke the twins again and again for being mean to me. Both boys loved it when they found out about my bedwetting and would tell anyone who came to the house. It was excruciating. When we were out and about I imagined people were looking at me as though I was some sort of freak. I could have killed the twins for betraying my secret.

Annabelle and Arthur would send us upstairs to play quietly together after dinner, but the boys would shut me out as soon as we left the table. Roland specialized in making hurtful comments. 'This isn't your house,' he told me early on. 'Go back to your own.' Another time, when he was feeling particularly spiteful, he said, 'Just because your mum's run off and doesn't want to know, it doesn't mean you can have ours.' The irony was that I didn't even want their mum. I wanted my own. Their comments hurt all the more because she didn't seem to want me. Of course they were talking about my birth mum, probably after picking up on some snippet of their parents' conversation. Yet another person who didn't want me, I thought at the time.

Gradually it dawned on my new foster parents that it wasn't working out. It all came to a head when we started getting into fights. I was two years younger, which should have put me at a disadvantage, especially given that there were two of them, but that wasn't how it played out. We foundlings were battle-hardened and quite dangerous when we wanted to be, with the result that the twins were constantly running off in tears complaining that I had attacked them. As their sons were usually the ones with bruises and red marks, Annabelle and Arthur were inclined to believe them. Soon they'd marked me down as a bully, always looking for a fight.

In a strange kind of way I welcomed the end of that Easter holiday. I knew that I was going back to a dreary routine and would have to live under the threat of even greater daily violence, but I was familiar with my world by then. I knew the rules. I accepted that the older boys had to be obeyed, but I never felt inferior to them or jealous. We were all in the same boat, having been abandoned, and we were all just trying to get through in the best way we could.

That break had been miserable from start to finish and I was actually pleased when I heard that Annabelle and Arthur weren't going to take me back. For the summer holidays, the school placed me with a childless couple who lived in the small town of Addlestone. Bert was a plasterer and used to come home covered in dust. I thought he looked like a ghost in an old black and white film. He was a rough diamond who'd been in the navy for a number of years, and it certainly showed in his weather-beaten face, which was wrinkly and craggy, almost like a walnut, and he'd made matters worse by falling in love with motorbikes and riding everywhere without a helmet. He told me that he'd seen a picture of Lawrence of Arabia astride his motorbike and had thought, 'If it's good enough for Lawrence, then it's good enough for me.' What he made of Lawrence surviving all those Arab revolts only to perish after coming off his bike in a quiet English country lane, I'm not sure.

Bert's wife, Elspeth, was a tiny woman, even smaller than Miss Pickles. She was timid, too, and looked a bit incongruous when standing next to her grizzled, six-foot-tall husband. They'd never had any children, and though I'm sure they thought it would be fun to have a little guy running about the place, they weren't really prepared for the reality. I asked too many questions, which seemed to annoy Bert in particular. 'Give it a rest, Tommy,' he'd say with a sigh. 'Can't you let us have a bit of peace?'

I got into major trouble quite early on when I was playing in the yard. Bert kept his bike propped up against the fence and I noticed one day that he'd left the keys in the ignition. I'd pestered and pestered until he'd taken me out for a ride – and it had been the most exciting thing ever. We'd roared down the road at high speed, my fingers gripping the material of his jacket as if I were a limpet clinging to a ship's hull, and when we took the corners, the wind whooshed through my hair so I felt as if I was flying. Looking at the keys now, I couldn't resist climbing onto the seat and firing up the engine as I'd seen Bert do, and with an almighty roar, the bike burst into life and lurched forward, crashing through the wooden gate which led out into the street. As the gate shattered into several parts, the bike fell onto its side with me trapped underneath. It was fairly heavy and I found that I couldn't wiggle my way out. I tried to lift the wheel and felt such a sharp pain in my lower leg that I cried out.

Bert had heard the engine and came rushing from the house.

'What have you done?' he cried. With biceps bulging he gripped the handlebars and heaved the bike off me. 'Are you hurt, lad?' he asked, eyebrows knitted in concern.

'No,' I replied, before looking down at my leg and seeing blood.

'Wait there,' he said and ran back inside. It didn't look like a deep cut but there was a lot of blood and I was pleased when he emerged with a towel.

'We'd better get you to the doctor,' he said, wrapping the towel around my leg. 'You never know what he'll find.' I presume he meant a broken bone, but luckily all was well and I didn't need anything more than a few stitches and a bandage.

Given that I'd destroyed the gate and left his motorbike – his pride and joy – with lots of scratches and a big dent in the side, Bert was very good about the whole affair. He and Elspeth told me off but they did it quietly while we sat at the kitchen table that evening. I hung my head and muttered about how sorry I was to cause such trouble, and they said it was all right but to be more careful in future. They didn't shout or threaten to hit me – and I marvelled, thinking how differently the Hospital would have handled the matter.

I was certainly much more content in their house than I had been with the twins. For a start, bedtimes were a lot calmer. The twins had made me feel so miserable and out of place. As soon as Annabelle had finished our story and put the lights out, they'd start up with their snide remarks. Worst of all, they'd poke fun at my bedwetting.

'Can you smell something?' Rod would sneer to his brother.

'Yes, now you mention it, I think I can,' Ron would reply. 'I think it's called "piss". It's coming from somewhere over there.' He'd point a finger in my direction and they'd both snigger quietly so as not to bring their mother back into the room. They were so sneaky and cunning, I couldn't retaliate without taking all the flak so I just had to lie there, burning with anger and shame.

I think Bert and Elspeth had been warned about my little problem before I arrived, because there was a plastic covering already on my mattress and I was given clean sheets every morning. Nothing was ever said, for which I was grateful. And it was heavenly to lie there at night with no noise: no snoring, no sniffling, no coughing, no chance of being rudely awakened to submit to some sort of vicious game. It was the first time I'd had some decent sleep in years.

During that holiday we went through a spell of very wet weather. Bert had gone off to work, Elspeth was busy in the kitchen, and I was at a loose end, unable to venture out. One of the areas of the house which remained a mystery to me was the attic, and I decided this was a suitable place to explore.

To get up there I had to climb a set of crude wooden steps which led from the first floor to a hatch in the ceiling. These were a little unstable and I found myself wobbling as I stretched my arms up to the hatch door. I steadied myself and pushed it open. It took a few seconds for my eyes to adjust to the gloom; then the shapes of boxes and old padlocked trunks started to come into focus. I decided these were definitely worth investigating, so I climbed the remaining two steps and hauled myself up with my arms. But there was something I wasn't aware of at the time – attics don't have proper floors. You have to step from one joist to another, and in between is a weak lattice with the plaster from the ceiling of the room below filling the spaces. This lattice is not designed to carry the weight of a human, not even a small seven-year-old boy. I gingerly took one step, then another, but on the third I heard a splintering sound as the plaster gave way and my legs broke through the floor into the bedroom below. As I plunged downwards my arms shot out so that I came to an abrupt halt at chest level.

Although I hadn't fallen right through, the crumbling of the plaster and splintering of the lattice had caused quite a commotion. It brought Elspeth running upstairs to find out what was going on.

'Oh my giddy aunt, what have you done now?' she wailed, throwing her arms up in the air and looking at my flailing legs. The air in the bedroom was thick with dust, which brought on a coughing fit.

'How am I going to get you out of there?' she spluttered. 'Are you hurt?'

'No,' I answered. 'I'm just stuck.' In truth my arms were beginning to hurt a little as they pressed against the broken lattice, but I didn't want to admit this. I felt such a fool, jammed in the hole with my legs dangling into the bedroom below.

It took a while to free me. First Elspeth climbed into the attic and tried to pull me up. She strained as hard as she could, but to no avail.

'Oh dear, Tommy. You're well and truly stuck in there, aren't you?' She wiped her brow and shook her head. 'Well, there's nothing else for it. I'm going to have to go to the phone box at the end of the street and ring for the fire brigade. Oh dear, what are they going to say? Whatever you do, keep still. I mean it, don't move. I'll be back in a jiffy.'

Twenty minutes later a great clattering of fire engine bells heralded the approach of my rescuers. On entering the attic the firemen stood astride two joists. One held me under both armpits while another hacked away at the plaster board around my chest. As the jagged lattice fell away, the fireman lifted me up and onto the joists.

'There you go, my boy,' he said. 'I think you've got a bit of explaining to do to your mum and dad. And you should thank your lucky stars you haven't got a big splinter of wood going through you.'

Sheepishly I thanked the firemen and began my descent from the attic. A very angry Elspeth was waiting for me at the bottom.

'Just look at this mess,' she said, surveying the wreckage of the bedroom, into which a large part of the ceiling had collapsed. The bed covers were peppered all over with debris. It was like a bomb had exploded close by. 'You are a stupid, stupid boy. How are we going to fix this?'

I'd never heard Elspeth raise her voice before, and it scared me.

'What were you doing up there in the first place?' she stormed. 'I wouldn't like to be in your shoes when my husband gets back. I don't know what he'll say.'

I couldn't think how to make it better so I just looked

down and shuffled from one foot to the other, trying to demonstrate as much contrition as I could muster.

For the rest of the holiday Elspeth made sure I was always where she could see me. Bert didn't shout when he saw the ceiling but he rubbed his brow in a weary fashion and I think it was a great relief to them both when they were able to put me back on the coach to the Hospital. It came as no great surprise when I found out that I hadn't been asked back for the next holiday.

17

Tom

A Dark Night

EVEN THOUGH I HADN'T been very well behaved during that break, and I could tell that Elspeth and Bert weren't best pleased with me towards the end, I had enjoyed the respite from the Hospital. For a few precious weeks, I benefited from the closeness and stability of a normal home life. Mealtimes were especially enjoyable. There was as much food as I could eat and, even better, I didn't have to stay silent while we were at the table. Bert used to speak about his day and ask Elspeth about hers and they'd both talk to me about the school. It was really nice.

Returning to the Foundling Hospital wasn't fun. It was always hard to settle back into the routine of the place after a break, but that term was particularly stressful as our housemaster, Mr Dumbleton, decided that he'd start reading us a bedtime story. I'm sure he had the best of intentions, but his tastes weren't conducive to a good night's sleep. Turning the main light out, he would sit at one end of the large oak table that ran down the centre of the dormitory and light a candle. There, in the flickering glow, he would read from a collection of Edgar Alan Poe's most terrifying tales. The contours of his bony face took on a sickly sheen in the half-light and I wished I could pull the covers up to shield my eyes from the sight of him. There's one tale that will be forever burned into my memory: 'The Pit and the Pendulum'. It describes a prisoner's experience of being tortured and plays on the senses, so that we found ourselves jumping over every little noise. I'm sure it inspired so much fear in us because we'd lived through pain and torment nightly at the hands of the monitors, so we believed that such terrible suffering was not imagined but real.

Tensions rose further when a foundling boy stabbed one of his tormentors. I knew him quite well even though he wasn't in my dormitory, and I think he just snapped one night, unable to endure hearing his name called out yet again by his sadistic monitor. He disappeared after the incident and was never heard from again. I can't see how the masters and governors can have failed to be appalled by the boy's violent action – and the bullying that provoked it – but still, not much seemed to change; the nightly crimes continued as before – and so did the sleepless nights, bedwetting and biting of nails. I tried very hard not to bite mine. We were constantly being ordered to hold up our hands to prove they were clean, and if they weren't we would be forced to scrub them with carbolic soap. I felt so sorry for the nail-biters; their poor fingers used to sting like crazy.

One good thing did happen to me that year: I was chosen to correspond with a woman in California. Marjorie Thomas was British by birth, but while she was serving as a nurse on the Western Front during the First World War she had met and married an American serviceman who took her home to California and proceeded to become a very successful businessman. Marjorie had read an article about the Foundling Hospital in *Picture Post* magazine and decided that she wanted to befriend one of its children. I still don't know why the Hospital picked me. With over six hundred pupils, it must have been a difficult decision. Perhaps it was because my name was Thomas – as was Marjorie's – and it was our founder's name too. However, there was another Thomas in the school and he was at an age to write more thoughtful letters, so perhaps the authorities felt that Marjorie's interest might make up for all the problems I was having with foster parents.

Whatever the truth, Aunt Marjorie – as she came to be known to me – proved herself a most wonderful benefactor. She wrote such interesting letters and in the loveliest handwriting too. My favourites were the ones she used to write from her holiday cabin in the mountains of British Columbia. She and her husband would motor six hundred miles north to the Rockies once or twice a year, and she

Left Aged three, with my foster sisters, Monica and Janet, in Saffron Walden. Janet was older than me but tiny for her age.

Right Elsie looked after me until I was almost five years old.

Left My father, Raymond, with his mother in one of her many fur coats.

Left My mother, Jean, with her first husband, Hugo, when they married in 1939.

Below Raymond serving in the Gold Coast – present-day Ghana – during the Second World War.

Below Raymond married his second cousin, Audrey, when he came back from Africa in 1947.

Left Jean with her second husband, Duncan Mackenzie, their daughter Katherine (*left*) and Maida, her daughter with Hugo (*right*).

Right This portrait of Captain Thomas Coram was painted by William Hogarth in 1740, a year after he finally obtained a royal charter for the Foundling Hospital.

Below A view of the original Foundling Hospital in Bloomsbury, London, 1756.

A View of the Foundling Hospital

Above The new purpose-built Foundling Hospital in Berkhamsted opened in 1935 and was my home from 1944 to 1954.

Left The infants used to march everywhere in crocodile fashion.

Left In my early years at the school, girls and boys were segregated. We used to attend chapel with the girls but were made to sit on separate pews.

Above George and Bessie with their marvellous cocker spaniel, Taffy.

Below George and Bessie look on as I prepare to put my swimming lessons to good use.

Left Aged eleven, on a day trip to the seaside with my friend, Nicholas (*right*). He was the son of the optician who gave me a job when I left the Hospital.

Right Aged fifteen, preparing to leave the Hospital and start work as a photographer's assistant.

Below Playing tennis with a friend (*right*) during my final year at the Hospital.

Right Working as a runner for a photographic news agency in Fleet Street, aged seventeen.

Left On parade with the 15th/19th The King's Royal Hussars in 1958.

Right After a 110-mile charity walk during my period of National Service.

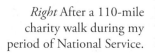

Left With my father in the early seventies, outside the health club I set up in Plymouth.

Below My parents, together again after a gap of forty years.

Left Celebrating my mother's eightieth birthday.

Below With my family. (*Left to right*) my son Ross and daughter Vicki, my wife, Ausra, and my youngest son, Grant.

would write of the beauty and variety of life there. The most riveting tales always involved the grizzly bears that made daily foraging trips to her cabin, and as she was obsessed by birds, she also wrote about all the hawks and eagles and grouse one could find nearby. But she admitted yearning for her homeland and the great variety of British song birds that so thrilled her as a child – noisy chaffinches and chirpy sparrows, melodious linnets, little wrens with their big voices and the never-ending notes of the song thrush. So vivid and emotive were Marjorie's letters that the Hospital adopted them for use during geography lessons.

The Hospital wasn't like boarding school; no one received birthday packages or postcards or notes from family members. I was the only one to get mail and I was always excited when a letter arrived all the way from America. Sometimes there were accompanying gifts too – mechanical toys and tasty treats that were impossible to obtain in post-war austerity Britain. Once she wrote to me to say that her son, Nick, a major in the US Marine Corp, was to make a visit to Britain in the course of his duties, and she had made him promise to look in on her little friend. My excitement was stratospheric and I told everyone about the glamorous visitor who'd be coming to see me. I had visions of the tall, sharply dressed major striding up to greet me before the envying eyes of the entire school. But the visit never took place. Perhaps his schedule was too tight, or perhaps he just didn't realize how much capital a little boy had invested in his visit. Marjorie wrote to say how sorry she was and that she'd given her son a real scolding for disappointing me. That pleased me a little – to think of the smart major having to submit to the wagging finger of his elderly mother.

Marjorie's letters were so lively and full of warmth that I've treasured and kept them throughout my life. I only wish I had shown more gratitude for them at the time. Marjorie wrote to me for several years and often mentioned how much she wanted me to reply and describe my life at the Hospital, but I found the whole business of writing desperately tedious and had to be continually badgered by the teachers to do so. I suppose it demonstrated a lack of imagination on my part. In the fraught years after leaving the Hospital at fifteen, with a bleak and uncertain future stretching ahead, I could have written to my wonderful benefactor and asked her to come to my rescue. A ticket to the sunny climes of California might have changed my life.

18

Tom

No Place to Call Home

School holiday after school holiday, I continued to move between foster parents. It seemed to me that nobody else in the Hospital was experiencing the same difficulties. Although one couple had apparently described me as 'a loveable little chap', they still didn't want me back, saying I was a handful to control. It was certainly true that if there was mischief afoot I would be there in the thick of it. The trouble over the attic was only the start. I was always getting into scrapes and having 'adventures' – much like my namesake Tom Sawyer, as one teacher delighted in pointing out.

One spring holiday I found myself back in the small town of Addlestone. My new foster parents were a pleasant middle-class couple called Mavis and Harry, who were nice to me but seemed slightly remote from each other. Harry worked in some sort of clerical post at the town hall close by in Guildford, and used to leave the house at eight fifteen.

every morning dressed in a smart navy-blue suit and tie with a trilby which he'd lift off the peg on his way out of the door. Mavis would carefully stow a couple of cheese sandwiches in his open briefcase before clapping it shut and handing it to him at the garden gate, then he'd turn his cheek, and she'd give him a little peck to see him on his way. You could tell it was a routine they'd been performing for years. They didn't seem to talk to each other much in the evenings, and I wondered whether they thought that having a foundling child about the place would inject a spark back into their lives – or at least give them a common interest.

I worried that Elspeth and Mavis might be friends, and sure enough, on the second day of the holiday, we bumped into her while out shopping.

'Oh hello, Tommy,' she said, looking somewhat surprised to see me. 'How are you?' Then, looking at Mavis, she said almost apologetically, 'I looked after him for a short spell last year.'

Fortunately they didn't seem to know each other that well and we were soon on our way to the butcher's, but it was an uncomfortable few minutes as I stood there hoping against all hope that Elspeth wouldn't mention the incident with Bert's motorbike or me falling through the ceiling. Perhaps she was anxious not to embarrass me or cause trouble – either way I was grateful to be given a fresh start.

It was a warm spring and I used to join the local kids

playing by the river almost every day. Despite my young age, I was already a very confident swimmer thanks to the Hospital's regime. We had a lot of fun and were never accompanied by an adult, which made a refreshing change. Looking back, it is extraordinary to think that such a scenario was possible, given how young we were. I'm sure there must have been scandals and accidents in those days, but the press didn't feel the need to sensationalize events as it does now, and our parents didn't bat an eyelid before sending us out into the world to play.

One day I joined a group of older children who were planning to explore the river upstream. We walked for a couple of miles, jumping in for a swim whenever the water looked especially appealing. When the sun was at its highest point we came across some boys from another village leaping off a bridge and into the cool depths of the river below and had an exhilarating time playing there for a couple of hours before heading off again. The day wore on and we just kept going until we saw a monument in the distance. It was Windsor Castle. Somehow we'd managed to walk all the way to Windsor – many miles from Addlestone and hours from home. By then our number had dwindled from around a dozen to four – and none of us had ever ventured so far. I felt a little panicky. Things had been going so well with Mavis and Harry, but now it was approaching dusk and I was out in the middle of nowhere. I knew they would be getting worried.

As it turned out, they were extremely worried. Harry had returned from work to find his ashen-faced wife frantically peeling potatoes. He later replayed the whole conversation so I'd understand how upset they'd been.

'What are you doing? There must be over twenty spuds here, Mavis.'

'Oh, Harry, it's our foundling. He should have been back long before now. I don't know where he is or what to do.'

'He's probably just playing. You know what boys are like – he'll just have forgotten the time. Have you asked the neighbours about theirs?'

'Yes, but that's just it. The neighbours' kids haven't seen him since lunchtime and they've all been back for hours now. They'll be tucking into their dinners and our little boy's probably lying at the bottom of the riverbed.' She burst into tears but wouldn't put the knife down and simply carried on peeling.

Meanwhile, the four of us who remained had to determine on a course of action. How simple life would have been had we lived in the age of mobiles, but not one of us even had a telephone in our own home so there was no such easy fix. We decided that the only way to find our way home was to follow the river – the same route but in reverse. I'm sure we could have made the journey shorter by cutting out many of the bends, but that required knowledge of the landscape – something we were evidently lacking since we'd found ourselves in such a predicament in the first place. Four hours later, and in pitch darkness, we finally reported in to our respective homes.

All hell had broken loose by this time. The police had been alerted and patrols were scouring the area for the missing youngsters. Mavis and Harry had been told to stay in the house in case I should return, and that's where I found them, sitting at the kitchen table – Mavis nursing a mug of warm malted milk and Harry a rather large Scotch. Although mightily relieved to see me – Mavis burst into tears and Harry muttered 'thank the Lord' – they were not best pleased with my actions.

I found myself grounded for the remainder of the holiday, forbidden to step beyond the confines of the house and its garden unless I was accompanied. Luckily for me it was at least a substantial garden, with fruit trees just beginning to blossom. There was also a shed with a large workbench where my foster father liked to spend much of his free time making things for the house, including a mechanized pulley to help Mavis with the washing, which I thought was absolute genius. It was fascinating to watch him, and occasionally he'd let me try my hand with one of the tools which made up his extensive kit. It was usually planing or sanding, though – nothing that involved a sharp object – and he'd hover anxiously behind me, ready to steady the implement or grab it from my hand before I could do myself a mischief. He was very patient and rarely raised his voice, but it did annoy me that he'd always take over and redo whatever it was that I was attempting.

As well as his workshop he had a greenhouse over which one of the boughs of the apples trees stretched. I'd been eyeing up that tree for a while and a few days before I was scheduled to return to the Hospital I decided it was now or never if I wanted to try climbing it. The first few branches were easy, but then, as I moved away from the trunk and inched my way along the bough hanging over the greenhouse, I heard a sickening crack. Before I could edge to safety, the branch on which I was sitting gave way and I crashed through the glass ceiling of the greenhouse onto the potted plants below. It was a catastrophe writ large – my greatest to date – and it brought a frantic Mavis rushing from the house to see what had happened.

'Oh my God, oh my God,' she screeched, looking at the mess of broken pots, shards of glass, plants scattered everywhere – and me lying in the centre of it all.

'What have you done, Tommy?' she said, picking her way over the broken glass and bending low over me. Then she saw the blood pouring from a wicked horseshoe of a cut in my knee which had exposed it to the bone. Quickly she turned and ran back into the house, her shoes crunching on the glass as she rushed to get some linen to bind up my wound and staunch the flow of blood. I would carry the gruesome scar as evidence of that misadventure for the rest of my life. Mavis and Harry must have been annoyed about the damage to their greenhouse but they were good to me and didn't shout; they probably thought my knee injury was punishment enough.

Never one to be deterred, I repeated the exercise at school a little while later. This time it was to be the Everest of trees. I would climb to the top of the tallest of all the giant cedars that graced the Hospital grounds. Cedars are notoriously difficult to climb for two reasons: first, long distances separate the boughs, and second, the spindly branches reaching out from the trunks have no flexibility and are liable to break suddenly. The upshot of this meant that while I managed to get to the top, I was soon stymied on the way down. It was a case for the rescue services.

In double-quick time – bells ringing – the fire engine turned out, along with the entire school. Up went the extendable ladder, higher and higher, until it was within a few inches of me. Then the smartly attired fireman, tunic belted extra tightly, shinned up and within a short time was standing alongside me.

'Come on, boy. Over my shoulder,' he ordered.

'No way! I'm coming down the ladder on my own.'

'Oh no you're not! You're coming down with me. Get over my shoulder,' he snapped rather sharply. I could see he meant business.

Fortunately, due to the wind high up in the tree, the

stand-off could not be heard by the assembled school eighty feet below.

'But you'll make me look such an idiot, and in front of the whole school!' I persisted. 'I'll never live it down. I'm ten times safer on the ladder than over your stupid shoulder. Listen, if I can get all the way up here on my own, I can get down your ladder. That's easy . . . please!'

But while all my arguments were sensible and undeniably true, they overlooked one small detail. Nothing and nobody was going to rob the fireman of his fifteen minutes of fame. Waiting below, among the throng, was a photographer from the local press, and I'm sure the fireman was anticipating seeing his picture in the next edition with some sort of 'local hero saves boy' headline.

Sensing the growing anger of my rescuer and fearing a lurch to grab me might precipitate disaster, I inched towards him and placed myself on his shoulder. Then, like a sack of potatoes and acutely feeling the indignity of it all, I allowed myself to be carried down. The humiliation was intense, especially when a great cheer went up as I was dumped on terra firma. I should have finally learned my lesson that day, but I'm afraid there were further climbing mishaps to come.

19

Tom

The Curtis Report

WHILE WE FOUNDLINGS WERE BUSY trying to muddle through those difficult school terms as best we could in the hope that we could enjoy a few pleasant weeks away from the Hospital during the holidays, there were political developments afoot that would transform the course of our childhoods irrevocably.

In 1946 Dame Myra Curtis and her committee had delivered a report which passed judgement on the quality of institutional care provided to children who, for whatever reason, had been deprived of a normal home life. Criticisms were levied against the harsh and repressive regimes in some institutions and the lack of any agency to whom the children could go to seek redress for their complaints. There was concern that the children were too regimented and lacked affection, particularly the younger ones who seemed desperate for attention and clamoured to be fussed over during visits carried out by the committee. It was also felt that negating individual identity was harmful to a child's development and too little effort was made to ensure the child reached his or her full potential. The Curtis Report concluded that institutional care was punitive rather than restorative and nurturing and recommended that vulnerable children should be fostered into families in the future.

The report turned the world of the Hospital upside down. The governors were made to realize that the way they had been treating us was all wrong. Even the style of the Hospital, with its hard parquet floors and panelled walls, wasn't suitable for bringing up children. The Hospital authorities had wanted to ensure that all surfaces were sterile as well as easy to clean, but they now had to accept that we might benefit from the comfort and warmth of curtains, soft chairs, carpets and rugs. After treating us like army recruits for so long, they finally came to appreciate that we were, after all, children, and needed love and affection rather than discipline and rules.

Having just constructed a brand new Hospital at vast expense, the governors decided that the best course of action would be to let the present occupiers run their course. I suspect the changes had been anticipated as there had been no new intake after mine in spring 1944. Year by year the numbers of children dwindled, and once I and my classmates had reached fifteen in 1954, the doors of the Hospital would close forever.

In the meantime, the governors realized that they would

have to set about the process of liberalizing their now condemned regime. It would start with a change at the top. The disciplinarian Mr White was forced to take early retirement and in his place, George Hodgson, a gifted mathematician from a top boys' school in Plymouth, was appointed. Originally from Yorkshire, he was a straight-talking Northern man who had a no-nonsense way of dealing with everyone – teachers and children. His wife, Margaret, couldn't have been more different. She spoke with the well-to-do tones of the home counties and was incredibly charming with a boundless level of energy. It would be needed in those first few months.

George and Margaret were installed in January 1949 in a fine large house called Braeside a few hundred yards down from the top of the steep hill on which the Hospital stood. They were separated from the other teachers who lived in smaller houses at the back of the Hospital, and this gulf in the standard of accommodation seemed to make some of the teachers resentful. I'm sure they must have regarded George as something of an upstart, one who was determined to impose a shakedown without considering the history and traditions of the Hospital.

First to go was on-stage caning during morning assembly. The practice continued in the classrooms, but George insisted that it should be on the bottom rather than the hand. The Curtis Report had criticized institutions for using uniforms to depersonalize children, and George quickly turned his attention to our clothes. He must have objected strongly to the girls' outfits as they were immediately allowed to remove their little white aprons and caps. The transformation was positive – they no longer looked like servant girls. Of course, uniforms continue to be used in state schools to this day, but the point is that these children can go home and change into their own clothes. They don't have to live with the stigma of dressing alike day in day out for their entire childhoods.

George treated us like people rather than recruits or skivvies. He put an end to most of our chores and it was a happy day indeed when we found out that we wouldn't be responsible for cleaning the Hospital any more. I'd spent so many hours mopping the floors of the never-ending corridors that I'd developed callouses on my hands. George also had all of our utility plates and bowls – made from hard enamel – replaced with pottery ones, and instead of having to eat in silence we were permitted to talk to each other. And for the first time, we were allowed to receive letters from our foster parents and to display a few personal knick-knacks beside our beds.

It was the most amazing change as far as we were concerned, but some of the long-established teachers were not taking kindly to George's reforms, and everything came to a head when George decided to ban classroom caning. He insisted that each teacher must bring the student concerned to his private study and administer the punishment there. This had a number of advantages. First, it was a subtle way of revealing those who were cane-happy as well as making them justify why such a punishment was necessary. Second, George was in a position to see that the punishment was carried out humanely, without an excess of enthusiasm. Third, the child would not be humiliated in front of his classmates. And fourth, no teacher wished to be seen as the one who really couldn't control the children in their class. As a result, the use of caning dropped markedly and became the exception rather than the rule, which is, of course, what George had intended.

This caused some of the teachers to complain that George was undermining their authority. They argued that the cane was necessary to keep the more unruly boys in line, and that as a result of George's reforms, these boys were talking back and disrupting their classes. A cabal of disgruntled old-timers mustered, and little by little they recruited some of the newer teachers to their cause. To make matters infinitely worse, the hardliners enjoyed the support of the Hospital's Secretary, Colonel Nichols, who was based at the London headquarters. Rumour has it that Nichols hadn't wanted to appoint George in the first place, but the governors had insisted that it was time for new blood and immediate modernization. Both men were determined to have their way over the issue of caning, so George made the bold step of going over Nichols's head and taking his case to the board of governors. One boy claimed that he'd heard the pair arguing in George's study beforehand – and reported that the Colonel was incandescent with rage as he accused George of threatening the traditions of the Hospital. George countered this by arguing that times had changed and the Colonel was too set in his ways. Apparently he then banged his fist hard on the table, but I'm not sure if I believe this. He was always such a gentle man and seemed to hate all forms of physical confrontation. Reason was his strength, and I'm sure that's how he managed to bring the governors round to his point of view. From that point on, caning was reserved for grave disobedience rather than little mistakes – and the classroom became a much safer environment in which to learn.

Although George won that battle, he hadn't won the war and many of the teachers – already vexed – were on the point of revolt when he insisted that they eat their meals with the children. Rescue came from an unlikely quarter. George's wife, Margaret, had noticed that almost all the opposition to her husband's reforms came from the male staff of the Hospital. A formidable woman with a gutsy can-do approach, Margaret decided to get the female teachers on side. She called them all together and appealed to their maternal instincts by claiming that such small children needed more than the basics; they needed affection, a degree of freedom and to be set a good example by their elders. If these children couldn't observe adults making polite conversation at the dinner table, how were they ever supposed to learn social skills? If they were always punished with the cane, how could they develop any notion of compassion, patience or empathy?

Before long the women of the Hospital had prevailed upon the men to ease their opposition to George's reforms. They had used the same masterstroke that the founder had employed two hundred years before: Thomas Coram, close to despair after so many years of fruitless campaigning to set up a home for London's abandoned children, had taken advice from his American wife, Eunice, who had suggested that instead of enlisting the hard-faced rich men of Georgian society, they should go after their wives. The women, including the King's own wife, were more than happy to sign Coram's petition calling on the King to grant a royal charter to the Hospital – and then, unsurprisingly, after much nagging, their husbands fell in line.

With the full support of his staff, George now set about a few further reforms, including allowing us to put a picture or poster at the end of our beds. Mine was Rembrandt's *Laughing Cavalier*, although I'm not sure why – it wasn't as if he was even laughing, hardly even a smirk – but I do remember feeling as proud as punch with my fine new exhibit. Wheels were also put in motion to allow us a little pocket money. There had been no point in this before as we were never allowed out of the Hospital and there was nothing inside to spend money on, but George saw that a tuck shop was set up as soon as sweets came off rationing that year. Unfortunately the nationwide demand for sweets and chocolate was so high that they were put back on four months later and we had to wait another three years before we could finally indulge our taste for soft nougat, sticky toffee, strings of liquorice and melt-in-the-mouth peppermint creams.

In my mind George's finest achievement was that he managed to put an end to the nightly abuses that had been going on for years. Rather than relying on the housemasters, who continued to turn a blind eye, he decided to stamp out the bullying himself. Shining his torch into the dark dormitories, he patrolled the Hospital for several months – frequently at first and then sporadically – but always turning up unannounced. The monitors never knew when he might make an appearance, and such was George's quiet stealth in approaching the dormitories that even the monitors' fabled 'skit keeping' system proved useless. Combined with this, the new regime was a chance for the bullying monitors to have a childhood just as it was for us, and I'm sure they didn't want to waste it.

If policing the dormitories was the icing on top of George's cake of improvements, then the cherry was turning the great hall into an occasional cinema. He had written to ask major distributors to loan films to the Hospital free of charge – and in the spirit of cheering us up, they agreed, so every now and then we were treated to a showing of the latest releases in our age category. It was an inspired idea and the teachers would often sneak some of their own children in for the occasion. As the lights were dimmed and the projector started whirring, there would be a great hush as we all gazed in wonder at the big screen. Those glittering Hollywood nights were among the best of my childhood, and for a few hours we could lose ourselves in a fantasy world altogether different from the one we occupied.

20

Tom

The Summer of 1949

As the weeks progressed towards the summer holidays that year, I began to worry about where my next foster home was going to be. The ones I'd gone to at Easter, surprise, surprise, didn't want me back, and from something my housemaster had said about smartening up my act before there was no one left to take me, I got the feeling that finding a home for me was proving difficult.

The Curtis Report had actually made my situation worse. Potential foster parents had to be scrutinized in far more detail than in the past. Children were not to be sent to homes where there was another child of the same age in case they played favourites, and nor were they to be placed in families without children. There were new guidelines stating that foster parents shouldn't be too old and they should preferably be middle-class rather than working-class. The Hospital had also determined to be more open in providing information about the children and their histories. I must have looked like a problem case with my bedwetting and my many mishaps, which were sure to put off most potential foster parents. They probably saw me as an accident waiting to happen.

All the girls had placements set up from the spring break, and by the time the summer arrived, the Hospital had succeeded in finding homes for all the boys who remained – except me. I wasn't aware of the frantic efforts going on behind the scenes to find me a home, and I just assumed that there would be one, so I lined up with everyone else to await the coaches as usual. My housemaster pulled me aside and told me to report to the school secretary's office, I wandered off to find Miss Brooks, thinking that she was going to tell me about my new foster parents and which town they lived in so I could get on the right coach.

Miss Brooks was about to leave her office as I arrived. 'Oh, hello, Tommy,' she said. 'Sit down and make yourself comfortable. I'm just going outside for a minute to help with the coaches but I won't be long.' Clasping a clipboard to her chest with one manicured hand, she pointed to a chair with the other. It was close by a window and provided a perfect view of the hustle and bustle going on outside.

This was the first time I had had any dealings with Miss Brooks. I knew she was an important lady who was in charge of all the school administration, including the day-to-day finances, and her office was close by the headmaster's in the area adjacent to the quadrangle where no children were ever allowed. I turned my attention from the excited children outside to the room. It was wood-panelled, as you might expect. Outside her office, on a wall in the large reception area, there was a plaque which read: 'They may forsake you but I will never forsake you.' I wasn't sure whether this was a message from our long dead founder or one from the Almighty himself. Either way I suppose it was intended as a comfort to us and had been a kind, even touching gesture by the designers when they had built the splendid new Hospital.

Miss Brooks had been gone ages and I started to worry. The fact that she had used my Christian name was rather ominous. I heard shouts from outside as my friends and classmates climbed aboard their coaches, and one by one the coaches pulled away and headed off for the summer. When the last one finally departed I burst into tears. There wasn't another soul in the quadrangle which minutes before had been a hive of activity. The truth was out there in that empty quadrangle. No one was willing to take me on. *What was so wrong with me?* I thought to myself. I hadn't been wilfully naughty or cheeked any of my foster parents, and apart from once or twice with the twins, I'd never shown any sign of a temper. When things had gone wrong, it was by accident rather than design. If only they hadn't gone wrong on such an epic scale.

Just then, as the misery of my situation was becoming

fully apparent, Miss Brooks came back into the room. She saw me hunched up in the chair and came over and put her arm round my shoulders in what I can only describe as a motherly way.

'There, there,' she whispered, pulling me into her. 'There's no need to cry, Tommy. You're going to have the best holiday of any of them.' I was too upset to listen. I felt bad about crying in front of her but I couldn't seem to stop. I was going to be left behind, the only boy in that huge empty school. Who was going to take care of me? Would the cook be forced to remain to serve me meals? That would surely make the cook angry. It was bad enough being unpopular with foster parents and now I was going to be unpopular with the staff, too. How, I asked myself, would I pass the weeks ahead?

Miss Brooks pulled a chair up in front of mine so we were facing each other. Then she took out a white hand-kerchief from her bag and reached forward to wipe away my tears.

'Now what you have to understand, Tommy, is that none of this is your fault. You were just unlucky. It's us grown-ups who are responsible. There have been so many changes since that wretched Curtis Report came out that we don't know whether we're coming or going. We're in a terrible muddle, Tommy, and you have been caught right in the middle of it. That's why I don't want you upsetting yourself.'

'But what's going to happen?' I whispered, trying not

to burst into tears again. 'I can't stay here all on my own.'

'No, of course you can't, Tommy, and you won't'. She smiled reassuringly as she finished mopping me up. 'There now, that's better, isn't it?'

I wasn't so sure but nodded anyway.

'You're going to have a fantastic time – better than any of your friends. You're going to stay with Mr Hodgson and his wife in their lovely big house and you'll be able to play in their beautiful big garden. Now, tell me you're not lucky. It's going to be amazing! You'll have the time of your life, I promise you.'

I didn't know what to say. I was pleased that I wouldn't have to spend the whole six weeks by myself in the Hospital, but what would life be like with Mr Hodgson? Better than with the former headmaster, Mr White, that's for sure. Just the idea of having to spend a few weeks with him was enough to send shivers down my spine. But Mr Hodgson had ended the bullying and he'd allowed us to chat while we ate. He had even introduced us to the magic of cinema. And his wife seemed lovely; she always had a smile on her face and a spring in her step. The more I thought about it, the better I felt. Perhaps Miss Brooks was right and I would have a good time after all.

George and Margaret had one child, a girl called Jane who suffered from a severe disability and wasn't in good health. It seems likely that their experience of caring for Jane – and in particular the patience they must have learned over the years – helped them to persevere with me. I tried my best to stay on the straight and narrow for the entire holiday and was relieved at the end of it that there had been no mishaps or injuries – not even a scraped knee. I was certainly my usual inquisitive self, which must have been tiring at times, but George and Margaret were easy-going and happy to allow me the run of the place.

For those few weeks I really felt like I was part of the family. We would take trips in George's motor car to Whipsnade Zoo or to see members of Margaret's family. Sometimes the journey would take an hour or more, and I couldn't believe how many twists and turns there were in the country lanes. How George was able to navigate his way through and around them, I'll never know. I loved pootling along with the windows down, the wind whooshing through my hair. Margaret would often tie hers back with a pink scarf and I thought she looked incredibly glamorous, like a siren from the silver screen. We'd also go walking over the Dunstable Downs, part of the beautiful Chiltern Hills, and if we were going to be there all day, Margaret would lay on a picnic spread. There were cucumber sandwiches on soft white bread, always with the crusts cut off, rosy apples and sponge cake with strawberry jam. Everything was delicious but the cake was my favourite. Once I ate three slices and felt a bit ill on the walk back to the car.

The world began to open up for me in so many ways.

I'd lived in Berkhamsted for a few years but I'd never walked along the old streets of the market town or visited the castle. George saw how much I loved getting out and about and would send me off to fetch him a pack of cigarettes from the shops. He smoked like a chimney and would get through two packs in a day. It seems extraordinary now that I would have been allowed to buy these, but that's how it was then. George would write me a note to say that all was in order and the old shopkeeper would trust that it was so. He took me to the castle as well. It was built at the time of the Norman Conquest in the eleventh century, and there were some interesting ruined battlements and a moat to play in. I used to imagine I was a medieval knight defending my fortress from enemy invaders and I'd swish my sword this way and that, cutting down all who came at me.

Life seemed to speed up that holiday. I remember watching the mighty steam locomotives which hurtled through Berkhamsted nearing the end of their long journey to London from Scotland. I was fascinated by them and George would let me stop in the middle of the bridge just as the train was about to go under. I'd get enveloped in steam while he would wait with a grin on his face at the end. We'd also mooch along the Grand Union Canal and observe the bargemen and lock-keepers at work. If I asked nicely they'd let me help to open and close the gates – and it was such a thrill to see the water rise and fall between the locks. I wanted to dive into the shimmery water more than anything, but I couldn't risk annoying George. In later years, when the rules about leaving the Hospital had been relaxed, my fellow foundlings and I would sneak off to swim in the canal. I was willing to take whatever punishment came my way for the chance to swim alongside those colourful exotic boats.

Every morning I used to emerge from George and Margaret's house and look up at the great pile of the Hospital – now empty – with its forbidding iron gates and high fence. I was finally on the outside and I didn't want to go back in. But all too soon the holiday came to an end and I had to contemplate the start of a new school year. First the small matter of my return had to be managed so that the other children wouldn't know where I had been. It was a cunningly crafted affair. I had pleaded with George to let me stay in the house for as long as possible, but he reasoned that it would look rather strange if I was seen walking along the road towards the school, so he gave me a book to read and placed me in the corner of his study, away from the window where the children might have caught a glimpse of me as they arrived by coach. Everyone seemed too preoccupied with their return to care about me when I emerged, which was just as well because spending a school holiday with the headmaster would have earned me endless ribbing.

I didn't breathe a word to anyone about where I'd been in the days and months that followed, but to tell the truth, I was sorely tempted to have a little brag. For my peers it would have been a really, really big deal.

21

Tom

A Home at Last

THOSE LONG HAZY SUMMER DAYS gave way to an extremely cold winter, the bitterest I had ever known. The temperature dropped to minus 20 °C and snow fell consecutively for many days. Paralysis seized the country. I began to worry about the Christmas holiday and what was going to happen to me. George and Margaret had offered to have me if no other home was available, but surely it wasn't proper to show such favouritism. I was certain it couldn't happen again – the governors wouldn't like it one little bit. But what if the Hospital couldn't find any foster parents willing to take me? How could I possibly bear to stay alone in the Hospital, especially when it was so bleak outside?

Luckily the reforms continued to raise my spirits. One very exciting development was that the town's flamboyant barber Percy Pocock was invited to cut our hair. Previously anyone and everyone in the Hospital had had a go and we used to end up with scruffy crew cuts and lots of painful nicks all the way along the hairline. You could tell Percy was a professional. He brought a collection of scissors, clippers and blades with him and used one of those soft brushes to swish the hair away from our necks when he'd finished. We trusted him implicitly, even though he was completely bald himself, and at the end of one haircut I summoned the courage to ask him whether he could tell which among us was going to end up bald like him. As hair was his trade, I thought he was bound to know.

'Ah, now there's a question,' he mused, scratching his shiny hairless pate for a few moments. Then he suddenly pointed at a few of us in turn. 'You, you and you,' he cried. When the shock registered on our little faces, he roared with laughter.

'I honestly don't know, lads,' he said, still chuckling. 'If I had the answer to that one I wouldn't be cutting your hair. I'd be Berkhamsted's millionaire ex-barber!'

I didn't know anything about my real parents and this meant that I didn't know lots of important details about myself, like how tall I would grow and whether my pale skin and sandy hair would ever darken. I used to wonder whether I'd be able to grow a beard, and of course whether I'd end up bald as a coot like poor Percy. As it happens, I did – although I don't suppose it would have helped to know about it then.

With us all looking so presentable and a great deal happier than when he had arrived, George decided the time was right for a school photo, something that had never happened before: each foundling had passed from babyhood right the way through to adolescence without a record of how they looked or how they had changed over the years. Margaret had given George the idea. While she was combing my hair during that wonderful summer holiday, she remarked how sad it was that all the kids were growing up without even a snapshot to mark their journey through childhood. An engaging and industrious woman, Margaret always seemed to have some scheme or other on the go; this became her next one – and George knew he wouldn't hear the end of it until he'd taken action.

That first photo was followed up by another a few years later – and it was marvellous to see how much we'd all grown. I treasured them for years, and even though one has now disappeared, I still take the other out occasionally and put names to so many of those long-vanished faces. It would be hard to forget those boys and girls, my fellow foundlings. We shared ten years together, all struggling to survive the regime and get through what passed for a childhood as painlessly as possible.

Although George encouraged the teachers and masters to use our first names, we boys continued to use surnames as it seemed odd by this time to do anything else. In many ways they were part of our armour – a defence against the vulnerabilities of childhood. During all the years we spent at the Hospital, we were like islands, forging only the shallowest of friendships, trying above all to be strong, resilient, to take care of ourselves, and this wasn't going to change overnight even in George's new world. I guess we'd all been let down too many times to believe we could ever count on anyone but ourselves.

It was with great relief that I discovered a placement had been found for me that Christmas. I was destined to be a special case again, though, and instead of catching one of the coaches with the other foundlings, I accompanied a teacher to the headquarters of the Hospital in Central London. There, at the foot of the grand staircase, were my new, undoubtedly brave, foster parents. Their appearance came as quite a shock. George and Elizabeth Deedman were old – well into their sixties – and they looked rather frail, especially Elizabeth. How on earth were they going to cope with me, much less grow to like me? If I was a handful to their much younger predecessors, how would they manage?

Despite the Hospital's best efforts, it seemed that there were no more suitable candidates willing to take me on. Perhaps word had spread through the foundlings' dormitory towns of the holy terror called Tommy. The Deedmans had originally applied for a girl, but their application had been shelved a couple of years before on account of their age and because there were no girls available. In desperation the Hospital had reopened their file and managed to persuade them to take on a wayward boy. As I looked at the kindly pair before me, I wondered whether they had been given the truth about my history. Maybe the Hospital had appealed to their Christian sentiments or pushed a sad, hard-luck story about my being the only child with no home to go to. I'll never know the answer to that, but somehow, against all the odds, George and Bessie brought my wanderings to an end. I would go to stay with them every holiday from the age of ten until I left school, and I came to know them as Ma and Pa.

I had some serious misgivings at first. George was a railway guard. He seemed to like nothing more than talking about trains or his beloved garden. He used to wheeze a lot, the result of being gassed in the trenches during the First World War, and he had the most extraordinary Roman nose and a bald pate exactly like a monk's shaven tonsure. The local kids used to make fun of him something rotten. Bessie was small and well turned-out, with a rather severe-looking Edwardian bun piled atop her head from dawn until dusk. They had never had any children and lived in a gloomy little house in Feltham, a town in South West London famous then for its market gardens and large railway marshalling yard. The house was shaped like an upended matchbox and had a lovely big garden, though no indoor toilet or hot running water. When baths were called for, George would drag a great galvanized tub in from the garden and place it in the centre of the kitchen.

Bessie would boil big pans of water and pour them in, one by one, until the tub was full. Clasping a sponge in her hand she would gently wash me, taking care not to get the suds in my eyes. To be looked after in this way was something new and very pleasant for me, but unfortunately it wasn't long before I grew embarrassed to be naked in front of my foster mother. The turning point came a year or two later when Bessie was drying me and passed the towel softly over my privates. I gained my first erection and she stared in utter astonishment. From that point on, and without a word being spoken, it was understood that I was old enough to bath myself.

I'm not sure whether it had anything to do with the lack of a functioning bathroom, but George and Bessie had neglected to care for their teeth and, like so many others of their generation, had paid the price. Each evening they would nonchalantly pop their dentures into a cup and I don't think it ever occurred to them that I would face the same fate unless they encouraged me to brush twice a day. When they were in a particularly light mood – which was often – they would take out their dentures to reveal the ugly gums and yawning dark caverns beyond and advance towards me at speed, clacking the disembodied pearly whites in their hands like castanets. I recoiled in horror. To see someone laugh without any teeth truly is a hideous sight. In later life I ended up having to endure a massive programme of restoration – fillings and veneers

– but thankfully, by waking up to the importance of brushing early on, I have nursed my set through to my seventies.

Life with George and Bessie was rather dull, especially that first Christmas when it was so bitterly cold that I hardly ever left the house. I used to entertain myself by reading a lot of comics about the adventures our soldiers were having in Africa. I got so caught up in the exciting illustrations and heroic mood that it never occurred to me that the trauma and financial strain of two world wars would bring an end to the Empire. Reading about tigers attacking red-coated British soldiers, and then later the exciting space adventures of Dan Dare, provided an escape from the sedate pace of life that George and Bessie so evidently enjoyed. They were affectionate with one another, though not touchy-feely (few were in those days), and there was none of the animated, educated talk that there had been at George and Margaret's. In fact, they talked very little, and what little noise there was seemed to come from the radio. They were fans of the comedian Arthur Askey and would also listen to Wilfred Pickles, whose catchphrases I can still remember: 'Give him the money, Barney,' and 'What's on the table, Mabel?' George used this line affectionately on Bessie when he got home in the evening. It would always make her smile.

But George and Bessie did have something in their home which interested me – their cocker spaniel, Taffy. I'd never had a dog before and was very excited. He took to me straightaway and would let me stroke and pat him till kingdom come. I loved it when he chased his tail and I was forever sticking my hand in to see if I could distract him and make him go the other way. That first Christmas, it was so cold that George would light the fire early in the afternoon, which meant that by the evening it was really toasty. I would lie on the rug by the hearth after dinner with Taffy snugly curled up next to me and we'd both drift off. Bessie would approach before long and pat me on the shoulder.

'Come on, Tommy, love, it's time for Taffy to go to bed now. Let's go up the wooden hill, shall we?' I was always reluctant to leave the warmth of the fire and George would sometimes have to carry me up. I was very sad when he couldn't quite find the strength in subsequent years.

Although I wasn't allowed outside to play that first Christmas, I could leave the house for Sunday school and shopping trips with Bessie, both of which I found very boring, perhaps more so than staying in where at least I could have played with Taffy or read my comics. George and Bessie didn't seem particularly religious so I wonder now whether Sunday school was a requirement made by the Hospital. The shopping trips were something that Bessie really enjoyed, though. She seemed to relish having me at her coat-tails as she bumped into first one and then another of her many friends. Then it would be clackety-clack, clackety-clack for the next ten minutes – which felt to me more like an hour – as she caught up on all the local gossip. It was truly agonizing and I used to fidget from one foot to the next, tugging occasionally at her coat. It didn't do much good, though, as Bessie never seemed to realize how bored I was.

As the years passed and Bessie moved into her late sixties, the conversations became more depressing as her friends started to die off.

'Oh, Bessie, did you 'ear what 'appened to Mabel?'

'No, Winnie, what?'

'Well she died, didn't she. On Tuesday night. 'Er angina got the better of 'er. Another bad attack. I can't think how Fred'll cope without her.'

I hated this type of gossipy report and used to mock the silly women in my head – *well, there couldn't be such a thing as a good attack, now, could there?*

Bessie was a kind woman and would get caught up in the drama. 'Oh, my, my! What a shame!' she'd say. 'Such a nice woman . . . such a nice woman!'

Not any more, I would think to myself cruelly as I tried to pull Bessie away.

Even more excruciating was when Bessie bumped into a friend who didn't know anything about me.

'And who might this be?' the friend would enquire, beaming in my direction.

'Well, it's Tommy, isn't it!' Bessie would reply, also

smiling. 'He's from the Foundling Hospital. His mother didn't want him so we're looking after him for the school holidays.'

'Well hello, Tommy. Isn't that wonderful of Bessie to have you, and especially at her age?' the friend would remark, with yet another smile.

And that was the issue. It was hugely embarrassing for me to be seen out with this old lady. Nobody could mistake her for my mum, so I presumed that people would know that I didn't have one and that I didn't really belong anywhere. I always felt that there was a stigma attached to going out with Bessie. It made me so unhappy, and seeing this must have upset her, too. I don't know why it never occurred to me that people might think she was my grandmother. That wouldn't have been too bad at all. I guess, never having had a grandmother, it just didn't enter into my thoughts.

The one good thing about these encounters with Bessie's friends was that they would invariably reach into their bags and, with another sweet smile, press a coin or two into my hand. Hateful though it was to stand there and hear that my mother didn't want me, I was always pleased to be given money. At the Hospital I had spent such a long time without anything of my own – no clothes, toys, books or games, or even food since much of the best used to be stolen – that to have money to buy sweets or to save and buy a comic was very exciting.

I'm ashamed to admit it, but a few years later, having never received any regular pocket money from George and Bessie, I took to stealing loose change from Bessie's purse, and worse, the purses of her friends while they were visiting. I knew it was wrong, and since every penny counted in those days, Bessie must have realized that something was amiss. She never confronted me about it, though, and nor did she complain about the bedwetting, which continued for some years. I can only presume she had grown sufficiently fond of her young charge that she didn't want to punish me or risk losing me.

George took a harder line and would chase me up the garden path if I exhibited any naughtiness. Luckily, at sixty-plus and wheezy, he was never going to catch me, so after a few attempts he gave up. I remember one particular summer's day he was furious because I'd blunted his favourite razor-sharp chisel. George had said that I could demolish an old cabinet, taking the screws and bolts out so we could later use the panels for firewood. I thought the chisel was a wide screwdriver and mashed it against the metal fastenings, turning the handle back and forth with all my strength. When George saw what I'd done he scrunched his hand into a fist and waved it at me menacingly, and I ran as fast as my legs could carry me and complained to Bessie. How was I supposed to know the difference? The tools looked just the same to me. Closer examination would have shown that one had a sharp edge and the other didn't, but little boys weren't into such subtle differences.

Small mishaps aside, George and Bessie seemed to really enjoy having me around. Bessie was a talented pianist and had been a music teacher in a local school in her early life. She was determined to teach me, but I was easily distracted and couldn't be made to sit still. I did love to hear her play carols at Christmas, though, and would always come running when she sat down at her stool in the evening. Although her fingers were gnarled and twisted with arthritis, she could still produce a fine tune and George and I would merrily sing along in the background, making up for what we lacked in talent with a hearty dose of enthusiasm.

George couldn't teach me anything about music, but he tried to impart the essentials of cricket. In the summer, he would don his Sunday best, along with his trilby hat and a gold pocket watch, the chain always dangling proudly, and he'd select one of his favourite walking canes and stride out towards the church cricket ground. Taffy and I would follow in his wake, playing fetch while he settled into a deckchair by the green and lit his pipe. There, puffing away, he would explain the finer points of the game to me. He always tried to cut as gentlemanly a figure as he could – not to impress me but to impress Bessie. She was an educated woman from a middle-class family and there had been quite a to-do when she had decided to marry George. Her father had fiercely opposed the match, believing that a railway guard wasn't good enough for his daughter, but Bessie had been adamant that George was her man – and he had spent his whole life trying to prove himself worthy of her love. Apart from their lack of success on the children front, the marriage had been a very happy one.

George used to rely on Bessie for just about everything. He'd give her his unopened pay packet each week on the basis that she was much better equipped to handle the household finances, and he'd ask for her thoughts on the goings-on in the country and where they should go on holiday. As George worked for the railway we were able to get free train tickets, so we used to go visiting quite a bit. They had relations in Worthing and we'd often go for the weekend. I think we went for the first time in the summer of 1950 and I shall never forget that amazing salty seaweed smell. It was my first visit to the coast and as much as I loved the countryside I couldn't help thinking how exciting it would be to get in a boat and sail away, just like our founder Thomas Coram had done two hundred years before.

Those weekends always flew by, probably because I spent so much time swimming in the sea. My skin would be wrinkled like a prune at the end of the day when George and Bessie made me get out and come inside. Like most young kids I was impervious to the cold. They were in no doubt about my abilities in the water by then, but the first Easter there had been a stand-off when I had demanded to go swimming in this huge gravel pit close to the house which had been filled with water and made an ideal pool. George didn't want to let me anywhere near it, but I pleaded and pleaded until eventually he gave in with a sigh: 'Oh, go on then, Tommy, you'll badger the life out of me at this rate.' He stood by nervously but I think he relaxed when he saw me execute the perfect dive – the Hospital's brutal pool introduction had done its work. Taffy liked to spend as much time in the water as I did and it made me laugh to see him paddling along, both ears sticking out and floating on the surface of the water. I used to hitch a ride on his back, kicking with my legs, and we'd motor to the other side. George enjoyed watching us in the water and he'd join in the fun by throwing sticks and seeing whether Taffy or I would get to them first.

Though the water was my domain, there was one area that George was totally in control of – his garden. It surrounded the house on two sides and was full of the most magnificent fruits and vegetables: red eating apples and big green cooking ones, pears, plums, peaches, black-currants and redcurrants, raspberries, loganberries, toma-toes, lettuces and courgettes, and in the autumn, cabbages, pumpkins and parsnips. Of all the bounty, George was proudest of his peach tree. His friends would ask how he managed to grow such outstandingly large specimens – they were unbelievably huge – and he would tap his Roman nose with his forefinger and refer mysteriously to having met some sort of expert a long time ago who'd given him some secret tips which he'd sworn never to divulge. It was a confidence he took to his grave. The sweet tangy taste of those peaches was truly spectacular. I remember biting into the warm flesh and the juices dripping down my hands. You can't buy anything like it in the shops today, and I only wish I'd made more of a fuss and demanded to know George's secret at the time. He might have told me. I was the closest thing to a son he had after all.

It's true that I wasn't the most willing of under-gardeners back then, though. From time to time I'd help out, but George gave me the grotty jobs. He'd want me to rush out into the street and collect manure from passing nags, usually the rag-and-bone man. I hated the chore, feeling it was unbearably demeaning to be seen shovelling up shit from the street, but it was too difficult to say no when George extended a sixpence for my trouble. He must've listened out for the hooves because he would always know when there were precious droppings to be had, and he'd urge me forward, thrusting the shovel into my hand. Clearly he preferred not to undermine his own gentlemanly status by running out to get it himself. Glancing up and down the street to see if anyone was looking, I would dash out and scoop the steaming shit into a bucket at lightning speed. Most of it was destined for a spectacular rose bush he cultivated at the side of his matchbox-shaped house.

Bessie would get very cross if I ever got any on my shoes. 'Oh, look at you, Duckie,' she'd say, 'you're not coming in like that. Clean them up before you go onto my clean floors.' I used to put on a scowl but I loved it really when she called me 'Duckie'. It was a much-used term of endearment in those days – and one I'd heard mothers use for their own children in the street.

Bessie's affections for me deepened as I spent holiday after holiday with her and George, and before long they said they would like to adopt me so we could be a proper family all the time, not just in the school holidays. All I had ever wanted was a home where I felt loved, and although George and Bessie were old and the holidays I spent with them could be very dull, I felt safe with them. Certainly, returning to the Hospital used to make me feel distressed and tearful, though I can't be sure if it was leaving them or the thought of what I was going back to that caused me to feel so miserable. It was probably a bit of both. But even though the idea that I might spend the rest of my childhood in their care was a pleasing one, I was determined to be cautious with my feelings, not knowing whether such a scheme was possible, or whether the Hospital would ever agree to let me leave.

22

Jean

A Cruel Choice

I HAD A MISERABLE TIME IN GLASGOW in the years following Hugo's death. Alone for much of the day with a young child and no one to talk to, I couldn't stop my thoughts returning to the life I should have had with Raymond in South Africa. I'd given up hope that my letters would reach him out there, so I decided to write to his mother – I just wanted to know where he was and whether he had been involved in the war effort. I needed to know that he was safe, that he was alive. Like all Empire countries, South Africa had joined the war, and I was worried about him, and to think that he might be among the casualties made me want to curl up in a tight ball and cry. But my letters to his mother went unanswered – out of spite or grief I could not tell.

In an effort to pull me out of my misery, my younger sister, Helen, asked whether I'd like to go on a date. At first I was disconcerted – I was in my early thirties with another man's child on my hip and another one from a relationship seven years before. I was hardly the catch I'd once been, and with so many young men lost during the war, it wasn't as if there was a shortage of girls on the lookout for a husband.

'Oh, Helen,' I said, taking my little girl out of her chair and wiping her mouth with my apron. 'Who on earth would want to take me out on a Friday night?'

'Duncan!' Helen replied, eyes sparkling with excitement. 'Go on, say yes, we can ask Mum to babysit, and it was Bobby's idea. He really wants you to come.'

Bobby was Helen's husband and Duncan had been his best man at their wedding. He had cut an exceedingly handsome figure in his Parachute Regiment uniform. They'd met at university and were both practising law now the war had come to an end. I remembered being impressed. My sister's offer sorely tempted me.

'Oh, really?' I replied nervously. 'I don't know, Helen. I'm really not sure. He probably doesn't even remember me. Bobby will have strong-armed him into it.'

'No, but that's just it, he does remember you. In fact, he's always had a bit of a thing for you. That's what Bobby says.'

'What?' I said, quite taken aback.

Helen smiled and came over to take my little one. I sat down.

'Don't you remember how he was looking at you at the

wedding?' Helen said. 'He was mightily jealous of Hugo that night, I can tell you!'

'I didn't notice. Tea?'

'Yes please, but don't change the subject.'

'I wasn't. But all right, you win. Tell me more about the dashing Mr Mackenzie,' I said, filling the copper kettle with water and putting it on the stove to boil.

'I only know what Bobby's told me, but apparently he, Bobby I mean, took Duncan to the pub after work one evening last week. "Guess what, my laddie," he said. "My missus has the most gorgeous sister you can imagine. You'll remember her from our wedding."'

I must have frowned because Helen rolled her eyes and said, 'Don't look at me like that. All right, I'll be serious. Bobby told Duncan about Hugo going missing in '43 and you being left alone with little Maida here. And Duncan replies, "Well, big deal. What am I supposed to do about it? And who's to say she'd even fancy me?" But you know what he's like. It's just false modesty. He's well aware of how handsome he is – and what a dash he cut in that uniform – the old fool. So Bobby tells him to stop messing about and gets him to agree to meet us for a meal in town.'

'Gets him to agree?'

'You know what I mean. You have nothing to worry about. Bobby told me that Duncan said his only memory of our entire wedding was "the bride's pretty sister" and how he thought it was such "rotten luck" you were married!

So how about that, then. Are you pleased?'

'Hmm,' I murmured, allowing myself the smallest of smiles as I took the whistling kettle off the heat and set about making the tea. It all seemed quite intriguing.

A week later, Bobby introduced us over dinner. Duncan was just as handsome as I remembered and there was an instant spark of attraction. It wasn't long before we were dating seriously, and after only a few months together, Duncan proposed. I was surprised but there didn't seem any point in waiting around – the war had turned everything on its head. So many lovers had been torn from each other that it seemed right to want to make the most of every single second together.

Despite the war making everyone a little less judgemental and a little more grateful just to be alive, I was still worried about telling Duncan about my situation. I needed him to make the same promise Hugo had to help me get my boy back from the Foundling Hospital as I didn't know if I could marry anyone without it. As luck would have it, the dashing captain, who could have had his pick of women at that time, wanted only me and was perfectly prepared to take on my children. He offered to adopt my daughter straightaway and would do the same with my little boy as soon as we were settled and in a position to support him.

It made me incredibly happy, but there were so many practical problems to sort out before I could think about trying to get my son back. I wanted to settle in a big city, preferably Glasgow, where my boy would be able to join us without setting tongues wagging, but when an offer came up for Duncan in the far north of Scotland shortly after we were married in 1947, I knew we had no option but to accept. With millions of demobilized men flooding the job market, he couldn't afford to be picky. And it was a good post – procurator fiscal (town prosecutor) in Dingwall, a small town at the mouth of the Cromarty Forth, just a few miles to the west of Inverness. Duncan was a highlander himself and I could tell he was pleased to be heading home. I was miserable, though, knowing that my boy, with his English accent, would stick out like a sore thumb there. I tried to comfort myself. After all, the most important thing was that Duncan had work. Once he'd established himself, he could trade on his good reputation and by then there might be more opportunities further south. In the meantime, we'd have money coming in and could start saving for a bigger house. The Hospital would require evidence that we could support Derek before releasing him into our care, and that would include providing him with a room of his own.

While all this was happening, Raymond – not that I knew this till much later – was stationed in the western Gold Coast – present-day Ghana – and had been offered the rank of acting lieutenant colonel. He had spent much of the war there, liaising with the RAF and arranging the assembly of fighter planes bound for the Middle East campaign against General Erwin Rommel's German Afrika Korps. The planes arrived crated and in kit form to be put together and flown the two and a half thousand miles across the empty expanse of the Sahara to Egypt – perilous work, since any pilot forced to crash-land or make a bailout would almost certainly die, but the necessity of avoiding the submarine-infested Mediterranean made the longer route a necessity.

Although he had enjoyed his experience of war, Raymond did not want to continue for long in the army once peace had been declared. His superiors thought this was a waste and offered to go firm on the colonel bait, moving him up from being a major if he agreed to stay on, but colonial tensions were rising by this time and Raymond had grown cynical about the whole business of soldiering and the future of military control in the Empire. With demobilization underway, he was as anxious as the next to return home to civilian life.

He had learned of my marriage to Hugo and told me later that the pain had been worse than anything he'd ever experienced. Though he was hurt by what he felt was my lack of faith, he didn't blame me, especially when he found out the circumstances; he even blamed himself to a large extent. Not only had he failed to deliver on his promise of a better life in Africa, but he'd also failed to keep in touch. I suppose we were both responsible in our own ways. If he hadn't been so proud and if I'd had a little more belief in his love for me – perhaps finding the courage to tell him about the pregnancy – we may have forged a life together. But hindsight is a beguiling thing.

When he finally returned in the spring of 1947, Raymond's family were keen to see him settled and happy as quickly as possible. His mother suggested a visit to relatives in the Birmingham area, the Batten branch of the family, among whom there was a very great beauty called Audrey, a second cousin to Raymond. It wasn't long before Audrey had fallen for him. A few visits more and the matter was decided: Raymond and Audrey would marry and move north to set up home in Glasgow.

I was married to Duncan and living in Dingwall by this time. I knew nothing of Raymond, nor he of me. We were both content in our separate worlds, each of us settling into the rhythms of family life in peacetime. I went on to have two children with Duncan – another girl and then a boy – and this made it difficult to think about moving south. Duncan liked to have me at home and I enjoyed being there. My place, I felt, was with the children. But this meant we were managing on one salary and there was no opportunity to put anything aside for the future. I really didn't know what to do for the best. Time was passing and my thoughts would often dwell on my lost boy, but after the tumultuous years I'd passed through, I had grown to quite like the quiet life that the little town of Dingwall had to offer. It seemed that every fourth person in that part of the world was a Mackenzie – like my husband – and I enjoyed feeling part of the clan, and to add to that, Duncan's job meant that we were invited to lots of social events and public functions. We were at the heart of the small tight-knit highland community, and my dilemma was that while I had been welcomed with open arms, I had doubts whether this welcome would extend to my son. There was still so much stigma associated with illegitimacy, and I didn't want to be the cause of any gossip that would embarrass my husband.

A letter arrived one morning as I was trying to give the children their breakfast. It looked official and I saw from the postmark that it was from London. My stomach lurched. It could only be from one place – the Foundling Hospital. I tucked it into my apron and hoped Duncan wouldn't notice my hands shaking as I sprinkled a little salt into the porridge.

I was worried that something terrible had happened. The Hospital never wrote except to answer my enquiries about my son's progress. All sorts of diseases were flying through my head: polio, measles, influenza, typhoid, tuberculosis . . . The worst thing was that when I finally sat down and opened the letter, for a tiny moment I wasn't sure whether to feel relieved or not. He was all right

– strong and healthy – but a couple wanted to adopt him, which would mean losing him forever. The Hospital wrote about the advantages of a happy home and recommended that I give my consent. I remember thinking that perhaps I should agree. How could I be so selfish and deny my son the chance to grow up with people who loved him? But then I wavered and thought how much I wanted him back. I yearned for him. For all these years I had refused to give up hope. Hugo's death had robbed me of a chance to reclaim my child, but I was married again now and I wasn't ready to relinquish the idea completely.

I thought about it for days, wrestling with my feelings and looking at my own three children. I loved them so much, and I wanted my son to have the same love in his life – but I wanted it to come from me. I didn't know then of the miseries he had to endure at the Hospital. All I could think was how final adoption would be; I'd never get him back, or even know where he was. I wrote to say that, after careful consideration, I was unable to give my consent.

23

Tom

Secrets Revealed

WHEN I LEARNED THAT MY MOTHER would not give her consent, I secretly felt pleased. George and Bessie were very nice and I had been happy to agree to the adoption, but to find out that I was still important to the one person above all in the world I wanted to know was thrilling. Somewhere out there, I told myself, was a woman who pined for me. It gave me a buzz beyond anything I had ever known.

The central tenet of the Foundling Hospital – one that went back to the very beginning – was that mothers and children should be kept in ignorance of each other. Mr Hodgson had implemented many reforms, but even he couldn't have brought about a change in this policy. The headmaster appeared to be very fond of me – after that first holiday he and his wife had regularly invited me to their house to play and occasionally for dinner – but he couldn't break such a major rule and tell me about my mother. He could, however, use his cunning to circumvent the rule.

Before discussing the unsuccessful adoption request with colleagues, George called me to his office and then asked me to sit on a chair just outside the door. Key to his line of thinking, I feel sure, was that few boys – least of all me – would be able to resist eavesdropping, particularly if they suspected the matter in hand concerned them. And of course he was right. I heard everything I believe I was meant to hear. I learned that my mother was called Jean and had married a solicitor named Duncan Mackenzie, and that they had gone to live in a Scottish town called Dingwall at the mouth of the Cromarty Firth. I was eleven or twelve years old at this time, and would carry these few snippets of information around in my head for almost a decade before – at a time and place of my choosing – I eventually acted on them.

His work done, George called me into the office to give me the 'sad' news that the adoption would not be going through. He then mentioned, without providing many details, that my mother had recently given birth to a baby boy whom she had called John and that she already had two girls called Maida and Katherine. As he looked at me with kindly eyes and patted my head on the way out, I found myself wishing the application to adopt had come from him and Margaret. They had been so good to me. In fact, when he later took up a new post in Kent, he persuaded my foster parents, George and Bessie, to let me come and spend part of each holiday with him.

Even though I counted myself one of the luckier foundlings – able to take care of myself in a scrap and highly thought of by the headmaster and his wife who had taken a shine to me – I still felt very alone.

Nothing made this more apparent than when a boy fell ill with polio. Everyone was gripped with panic as we all knew that polio was a highly infectious disease that often proved fatal. It had the capability to sweep through the whole school like the Black Death, or so Matron Grainger alarmingly declared to the teaching staff when she thought we weren't listening.

The poor boy was called Norman and he was in my dormitory. He was whipped off to the infirmary at double-quick speed, and when polio was confirmed, everyone in our dorm had to decamp to another wing of the infirmary for a three-week period of isolation. It was a welcome break from lessons, but my thoughts kept returning to poor Norman, who wasn't doing so well. We were allowed to visit him later on and I was shocked to see him lying on his back in what was described as an 'iron lung' – a full-body ventilator that was supposed to create negative pressure around the chest which would somehow help air to reach his lungs. He appeared cheerful enough and seemed pleased to see us, but a week or so after this, we learned that despite their best efforts the doctors hadn't been able to save him. He passed away without a single family member to mourn his loss. A little eleven-year-old gone to heaven, so they told us. My abiding memory is of him lying in that weird metal cylinder with only his head sticking out. It was a grim, depressing time and we were all affected quite badly, not just because we missed Norman but because his death seemed to highlight how very alone all of us were. None of us went to his funeral. Perhaps they thought it would be too upsetting.

No one else caught the disease. The Foundling Hospital had always prided itself on providing expert medical care for its children and the infirmary was state-of-the-art. In fact, surfaces in the Hospital – floors, tables, chairs, windows – were cleaned so often that they were probably close to sterile and this must have helped to contain the infection.

There were some problems that the Hospital infirmary couldn't deal with, though, and this would mean a trip to a real hospital. I had to have several operations at Moorfield's Eye Hospital in London to correct a squint that had been picked up by my foster parents, George and Bessie. My vision had been blurry for a while, but I'd been ignoring the issue and hoping no one would notice. I had a bit of a hard-man reputation at the Hospital, so I really didn't want to have to wear glasses – they would give everyone the impression I was weak and could be picked on. When

Matron Grainger finally clocked the fact that I really couldn't see properly and my eyes pointed in different directions, she said it would have to be an op. I was a bit anxious, but it was actually quite exciting to make a trip to London. In the end I had to have three operations because after the first two I peeked from under the gauze pad and let daylight in, thus ruining the surgeon's good work. Thank goodness the operations were quick and not too painful, although my eye was a bit itchy afterwards.

The third operation coincided with my eleventh birthday, for which the Moorfield's kitchen staff baked me a cake. The Hospital ethos had taught us never to cry, but I couldn't help myself on this occasion. I sobbed my socks off.

'What's wrong, Tommy?' asked one of the nurses, bending low to stroke the back of my head.

What was wrong was that it was the first birthday cake that had been made for me since Mum had made me one seven years before when I was four. I felt mortified that everyone had seen me lose control, but I was thankful that no one at the Hospital would ever get to know of it. The other boys would never have allowed me to live down such a lapse.

24

Tom

Growing Up

GEORGE HODGSON MADE GREAT HEADWAY in reforming the Foundling Hospital, but at considerable cost to himself: he had made an arch enemy in the Hospital's Secretary, Colonel Nichols, who opposed many of his new policies. Eventually George became so frustrated that he was driven to accept a headmaster's role elsewhere.

Yet George's reforms stood. Even Nichols, with his passionate defence of strong discipline as being character building, could not roll them back, nor could he turn back the tide: many of the recommendations in the Curtis Report were made law by the Children Act in 1948. The country had begun to recognize children as individual beings with individual needs, and this sympathetic approach had put a lid on Nichols's hard-line take on the matter.

I was very sad to see George go, especially as the Hospital installed a stern, stocky-looking new head in his place. Mr Gilbertson's principal aim was not to restore the old order but to raise academic standards. He did not buy into the centuries-old Hospital ethos that it was enough to teach the basics. To lend force to his intentions, he was to be seen striding with short, fast steps in a determined fashion around the school in full mitre and gown. The mitre had another useful application: it masked a bullet-shaped head that was completely devoid of hair. To further disguise this, he kept what there was close-cropped at the sides.

Still in his thirties, and a fluent German speaker, Mr Gilbertson had been an intelligence officer both during and after the war, with special responsibility for interrogating some of the top Nazis. Goering and his associates must have been not more than a little impressed that their enemy was capable of producing such a ferocious-looking and skilled interrogator; one quite the equal to anyone who came out of their own loathsome stable. He certainly cut a formidable figure as he strode around the Hospital in his flowing robes, frowning at any boy who looked like he might be up to mischief. He was stricter than George and definitely didn't have the same easy-going 'Let's stop and have a chat; tell me about your problems' approach that George had.

The two men did have one thing in common, though. Neither of them wanted to place as heavy an emphasis on religion as previous headmasters had done. Church attendance eased and there was a reduction in the number of hours devoted to the study of scripture in the classroom, which was quietly welcomed by us kids. At times the chapel had felt like a second home: we always seemed to be there, and while some of the hymns were uplifting, I found the sermons excruciatingly boring to sit through. There was a point at which I felt I knew the liturgy so well that I could have conducted the entire service on my own.

The downgrading of religion would have greatly saddened the founder. He loved the reformed Church of England and did his best to push it in the Thirteen Colonies of the New World where many of his trading interests lay. Religion had always played an important role in the formation of the souls we were said to have; it certainly left a firm imprint on all the children who passed through the Hospital's hands On the very day that my mother handed me over at nine weeks of age, the charity had summoned a vicar to its London headquarters to receive me into the fold. The name given to me by my mother was struck out and my new one substituted, and in that name I was duly christened. Thirteen years later the Bishop of St Albans arrived at the hospital in Berkhamsted and confirmed our batch as soldiers of Christ.

Ironically, the chapel was the centre of the only true scandal to hit the Hospital during my years there. The resident vicar became sexually involved with one of the boys and the pair ran off together, though 'run off' is perhaps not the right term, since the vicar was confined to a wheelchair after having been shot up in the water – so he had said – by the Japanese during the war. The boy in question had been spirited away in the vicar's car, and a nationwide manhunt, spearheaded by the *News of the World*, was launched to find him. It wasn't long before boy and vicar were apprehended – one of the police's less taxing manhunts, it was later quipped, since there weren't too many young boys with wheelchair-bound vicars about (especially one witless enough to continue wearing his dog collar). But after the scandal had made it onto the front page, the Reverend was not replaced.

My own memory of the Reverend centres mainly on the enormous strength in his arms; the result, no doubt, of using them for propulsion. This would be demonstrated on all the pretty boys who came within his reach. If anyone unwisely spoke out of turn, he'd seize them, pulling them onto his lap where only a penitent plea for mercy would grant any chance of release from the bull-like strength of his grip. Given the stories we now hear about abuse in children's homes, it is hard to imagine that the vicar's kidnapping of the boy was the only sexual misdemeanour that took place. With the code of silence being so deeply ingrained in the foundlings' psyche, it is, however, the only one that I am aware of.

There was one other figure who liked to capture us in his grasp, but in the case of Mr Tidey, the Hospital caretaker, it was purely platonic and all in good fun. His favourite weapon of intimidation was the fierce stubble on his chin and face. He seemed always to have about five days' growth, and any boy careless enough to come near would be grabbed by him and have the tender skin of his face drawn across Mr Tidey's bristle. It was a truly terrifying experience. The sudden appearance of that Desperate Dan-like figure of comic-book fame would see the boys scatter in all directions, laughing hysterically as they fled.

It was around this time that the Hospital began accepting day attendees in the form of local children from Berkhamsted. It was part of the process of liquidating itself, and as foundling numbers dwindled it was thought best to start preparing for the time when the premises would be taken over by the local authority and turned into a secondary school.

We saw a marked improvement in the quality and breadth of our lessons. For the first time we started to study science, which I found really fun, partly because we used to leave the Hospital and go down to the bottom of the hill to the laboratories. Once my entire class found itself choking with chlorine gas after an experiment went wrong. I also really enjoyed English, but I found examinations rather stressful and it took time to prove myself. Our classes were split into A, B and C, and I was in the B stream. There would be examinations in all subjects at the end of each term and this would establish our class position in each subject and our position overall in the class.

I think everyone found the whole business quite fraught, but my anxieties went beyond the norm – when put on the spot, as in my Maths tests, I'd often get a mental block and that would be it. As time passed, though, I began to feel less stressed, and after I was promoted to class A, I gradually climbed up the pecking order until, amazingly, on my very last exam sitting before leaving school, I came top. I cannot describe the euphoria I felt. It gave me a tremendous fillip as I left school, and I hoped it would help me to find a job. Like all the foundling children, I had no formal qualifications, but at least I would be able to say that I had been top of the class.

The strangest thing that found its way onto the curriculum in those final years was dancing. Someone, I don't know who, obviously thought that our life chances would be enhanced if we learned how to dance, so for a while it became the vogue. I had no interest in the steps or learning to be graceful, but, being in my early teens by then, I did like the fact that you were paired off with a girl. It was terribly embarrassing but secretly exciting at the same time.

Girls were largely a mystery to us. After all, we hadn't had a lot to do with them over the years. Lower down the school they had been a chink in our armour, since no boy would ever strike or tease a girl too much, no matter how brutally he treated his male peers. A little rhyme danced on the lips of every infant boy:

Sugar and spice and all things nice,
That's what little girls are made of.
Snakes and snails and puppy dogs' tails,
That's what little boys are made of.

It was only when George was appointed headmaster and he made it one of his priorities to end the segregation that girls became a fact of life. I was happy to see more of Janet and gradually we got used to spending time with the girls and they lost some of their mystery. But we were absolutely spellbound when a large number of new girls arrived from Berkhamsted as day pupils. They fascinated us in a way that the girls we had grown up with, albeit at a distance, could not. Their arrival coincided with the start of my own puberty and the talk became which of them was the most fanciable. A pretty face counted for more than the figure – though it has to be said we were mightily curious about the latter. Suddenly every boy wanted a girlfriend, although how to get one none of us had quite worked out yet.

The new boy arrivals might have been less interesting but their coming was just as noteworthy. There was quite a lot of hostility at the beginning and they often took us on in fights in which, to our disgust, we saw our sacred codes flouted. While we followed 'Queensbury rules', they seemed to adhere to the 'anything goes' idea and would kick at us, whether we were up or down, but they soon learned that they were no match for us dormitory-hardened boys. It only reinforced our contempt when they exhibited what to us was the most detestable habit of all, spitting. Then there was that ultimate manifestation of weakness, crying. It had been the time-old practice for us during fights that – however painful and great the damage inflicted – each boy had to maintain his composure. Not to do so would give extra satisfaction to the winner, and while you may have lost, it was important to avoid being seen as a victim – a 'cowardy, cowardy custard', as we would taunt to the snivelling new boys.

When we foundlings were taught of heroes – domestic and foreign – the greatest and most admired were the Spartans. We liked to imagine ourselves as their modern equivalent, a twentieth-century reincarnation, and would ask again and again to hear the story of how the vastly outnumbered Spartans defended Greece from the Persian invasion at the Battle of Thermopylae. The idea that so few could hold off so many appealed to us, and we made it our business to teach the effete boys of Berkhamsted a lesson or two in valour as well as chivalry.

It was after the town kids joined us during the running-down of the Hospital that a number of what might be described as bad habits crept in. One of them was smoking. It never really took off among our dwindling band, partly because of the money involved, and also because we were all put off when one of our boys was caught by the fearsome Scottish housemaster, Mr Homan, whose response was draconian. He made the boy smoke an entire packet of the strongest brand – I think they were Turkish. I've never seen anyone be so sick. The experience probably put him off the habit for life.

But there was another even stronger reason to avoid cigarettes. Mr Gilbertson was a chain-smoker, and within a few short years of taking up his appointment, at the age of only thirty-nine, he died – of lung cancer. The school gave him a kind of lying-in-state for a couple of days in the Hospital chapel, during which the choir sang a solemn requiem, and the sight of the coffin had a profound effect on me, as doubtless it did on the other children. It was the third time I had seen death at close quarters, the first being when my much loved foster father was taken from me, and the second when Norman had died from polio. I found it hard to get my head round the fact that the strident, hyperactive, bull-like Mr Gilbertson, with all his physical power and headmasterly gravitas, had gone. There he was, lying inert, and he would never say anything or do anything ever again. Life till now had seemed eternal, but here was proof that it was transient. With my time at the Hospital drawing to a close, I began to think about what would become of me, and how I would I fill the years to come.

25

Tom

The Earth Moves

At the end of the school day when lessons had finished and the Berkhamsted children had headed down the hill to their homes for dinner, there was a strange atmosphere, as though all the hustle and bustle had gone with them. I'm not quite sure how to describe it: surreal might be the word, or eerie. When I had arrived at the Hospital, there were around six hundred pupils. Now there were fewer and fewer of us each year as those who left where not replaced.

The day attendees must have thought it was absurd – just a handful of kids left to occupy a building a hundred times the size of their little homes, but if they were jealous of our palatial quarters, they didn't show it. They never stayed longer than they needed to and we were left alone to wander the endless corridors and do virtually as we pleased. There were still some rules, of course, but those fierce eyes that had previously watched over our every movement were nowhere to be seen. The barrack-like dormitories, the scene of our nightly miseries, now resonated with the sound of happy, playful voices. We would shout as loud as we could just for the joy of hearing the echo back. We would stamp our heels down on the hard parquet floors and make them sound like kettledrums. We even raced around the quadrangle, that once hallowed 'no-go area'. Now it lay at the mercy of our disrespectful scorn.

The whole dynamic of the school had changed. Having lived in fear for years, biding our time until we had reached the top of the pyramid and could lord it over the smaller, younger boys in our turn, it was a bit disappointing to be robbed of this rite of passage, but only a bit – the freedoms we were able to enjoy now more than made up for missing out on being kings of the castle.

There was a lot of time to fill once we were relieved of our cleaning duties and chapel visits, and in the summer, sports were top of the agenda. Although I enjoyed the others, my true love was cricket. I'm not sure whether this stemmed from all those matches George took me to see on the village green, but they must have contributed. I was a mean bowler, but I was useless at the wicket. Through all the holidays I spent with George and Bessie I never did get the hang of catching the ball properly. It's not that I wasn't good at fielding – I could take a catch out at the boundary or close in at the slips. The problem was that I couldn't seem to absorb the impact of a fast-moving ball by allowing my arms to go with the flow. Instead, I'd block its travel so it would smash against my hands as though colliding with a wall. They used to sting like crazy at the end of a match: it was almost as bad as being caned. It's such a shame that George never got to come and watch me play. He would have loved to see the fine pavilion and the immaculate grounds, and it would have been great to have had someone cheering me on from the sidelines.

In my last year or so, they fixed up tennis nets in the spacious grounds and supplied us with racquets and balls, but unfortunately no wire enclosure – maybe funds were running low at that point – so every time my opponent played a winner, I'd have to run half a mile to recover the ball. It was tiring work, even with the benefit of young legs.

In those last few summers, we were free to make our own pleasures. I won't forget the first time we were allowed to leave the Hospital grounds – it was so exciting to roam around without anyone keeping tabs on us. We used to wander for hours and our forays would take us into some of the most fabulous landscapes England has to offer, the Chiltern Hills among them. There was a mysterious wood we used to delve into in the hope of finding the one particular part where wild raspberries used to grow. It must have been unusual because, while blackberries in England are two a penny in season, raspberries are not. They were expensive to buy even then. But there, in that special place, we used to gorge ourselves to our heart's delight.

We had money in our pockets, as the Hospital had started giving us a little, and we looked for ways to spend it. One of them was to go to matinee performances of the movies on a Saturday morning, which cost sixpence, known then as a tanner, though we worked out a dodge whereby one of us would pay and go in and then open the fire exit door to let the others sneak in for free. But even with pocket money, we were never going to be able to afford one of the things we envied most about the lives of the town children – their bikes. Most of the Berkhamsted kids had them, so we took to scouring the town's refuse tip – the 'dump' as we called it – for a mix of rusting and broken bicycle parts to bring back to the Hospital. There we would set about a labour of love. Many, if not all, of the parts were in a truly dreadful state – rusty, bent, seized up, you name it; but miraculously, after hours of hard rubbing and restoration, those wheels, handlebars, pedals and twisted frames were assembled into working bikes. Each was painstakingly painted into a high gloss and christened with a colourful transfer. Mine was a devil, and, being red, became known as the Red Devil. We must have found a huge number of parts at that dump because we managed to put a lot of bikes together – a veritable fleet of them – and as we foraged, we came up against rats, lots of them. Each of us was armed with an iron rod so that we could deal with them – it was exciting and scary stuff, and on one occasion when the friend I was with wasn't fast enough, the rat got in first with a bite. We had to lie to matron about what had happened in case she wouldn't let us go again.

Learning to ride the bikes was a small matter – ours was always a can-do approach. We were ready for anything and just catapulted ourselves into the saddle and pedalled like crazy. It paid off, though there were a few nasty pile-ups along the way. We took to the roads of east Buckinghamshire and west Hertfordshire, and in a three-month period, which is probably how long the good weather lasted, learned more about the world beyond the Hospital than we had discovered in the previous eight years. A favourite ride was to the small town of Chesham, just a few miles across the county border. The final approach took us down a long steep hill, on which we achieved frighteningly high speeds. How none of us ever came a cropper I shall never know. Brake maintenance was entirely down to us, and since none of us was a trained mechanic, it was likely the brakes were decidedly iffy.

As it happens, I did have a major accident a bit later but this had less to do with brakes and more to do with my absorption in the film I had just seen. I was staying with George and Bessie and had decided to cycle to the town of Staines, which was four or five miles away, to see

Bridges at Toko-Ri. I can still remember that film – it starred Hollywood legends of the time William Holden, Grace Kelly, Mickey Rooney and Fredric March – and it featured a US navy pilot who had to bomb some heavily defended bridges in the Korean War. It made a powerful impression on me and I could feel the adrenaline coursing through my veins as I pedalled furiously home, head down over my drop handle-bars, dreaming of Hollywood and oblivious to the world. I obviously wasn't paying very much attention to the road as I ploughed straight into the back of a parked car. I was out for the count with what turned out to be concussion. I don't even recall getting home. It wasn't in an ambulance, I know that, but Bessie did call the family doctor and I spent the next two or three days in bed. Nowadays, I would have been rushed to hospital for a CAT scan and blood tests – the works. Helmets weren't worn as they are today, and if I had been wearing one, I would probably have escaped concussion altogether. It's amazing how cavalier we were to danger in those days.

We chased thrills wherever we could, and after those super-speedy races down the hill into Chesham we'd make a beeline for the local Woolworths to test our nerve by nicking sweets and small toys, and, for some reason, ties. They were the most sought-after item. You'd think we would have had enough of uniforms by that point. Thankfully we never got caught.

We were always after free stuff. One Sunday morning before church we decided to raid a local cherry orchard. After stuffing the pockets of our 'Sunday Best' suits, we began the hectic ride back along the twisting lanes to reach the chapel in time for morning service. Eating the cherries as we furiously pedalled along, the lead riders took to twisting round to spit the pips at those behind. Suddenly one of the leading bikes lost control and crashed to the ground. Within seconds, fifteen or more bikes lay in a twisted heap on the road. Dozens of crushed cherries disgorged their dark red juice, staining every one of our light grey suits, and when we parked our bikes and burst in for morning service, all faces turned to stare at our blood-red attire. It was just as well the Hospital regime had eased. Under the draconian headmaster, Mr White, such disrespect, especially to the almighty, would have merited a mass caning next day at morning assembly.

In spite of all our success in recovering parts, we still needed money for odd bits and pieces such as nuts, bolts, emery cloths and paint, so we looked for means to boost our pocket money. I hit on the idea of visiting the local golf club and pretending we knew all about caddying. Off I went with my friend Fred Jacks, and we loitered outside, trying to push our chests out and our shoulders back to look strong.

'I take it you've done this before?' enquired the man who first took up my offer.

'Yeah,' I replied nonchalantly, 'loads of times.'

'Grab that bag, then,' he said. I picked it up and winked at Fred, who had been assigned to the man's friend.

What a fool I made of myself that day. When the man struck the first ball I rushed off down the fairway after giving out a whoop. 'I've seen it, I've seen it!' I hollered. When I reached the ball, which had rolled off into a small area of scrub, I picked it up and waved it aloft triumphantly before running back at top speed to the astonished players.

My patron looked at me disdainfully. 'I thought you said you'd done this before. In fact, weren't your exact words "loads of times"?'

I looked from him to his friend, who was doing his best to supress a smile, and then down at my feet. I felt really stupid. Fred, who was standing next to me, cracked me on the ankle with his shoe. He went right for the tendon, where it would hurt the most. There have been few moments in my life where I have felt so utterly foolish and humiliated.

As we made our way down the fairway, awkwardly carrying the heavy bags, Fred whispered in my ear. 'You bloody fool, you've made us look like total idiots and liars.' I was mad at him for taking this line. It could as easily have been him. Perhaps he did know a tad more than me – at least about not picking up balls – but he was just as stumped when his man called for the 'driver'. He had no idea what a driver looked like and fumbled away until his patron lost patience and grabbed one from the bag. I saw the panic in his eyes and drew more than a little satisfaction from this.

That, understandably, was our one and only attempt to raise money by caddying. In desperation we took to cadging from people on the street – begging, in plain language – telling them we were from the Hospital at the top of the hill and hoping they would feel sorry for us and give us a few pence. Some did, but the experience was too humiliating so we soon gave it up.

26

Tom

Girls, Girls, Girls

SUMMER CAMPS WERE FIRMLY in the tradition of the Hospital. Although they were suspended for the war and its aftermath, by the time I joined the upper school the country was returning to normal and we were once again allowed to camp out under the stars. Before George Hodgson's reforms, the annual camp was a much awaited and exciting interlude in the otherwise grim daily routine. The teachers were around day and night, so the dormitory bullying proved hard to maintain out in the field.

While spending time in the great outdoors – running around and playing games – was a lot of fun for us kids, I don't think pleasing us was the primary aim of the camp. The holiday to me, at least, seemed more like preparation for military training. We learned the arts of field craft and tying complicated knots, and caught rabbits before skinning and cooking them. I knew a thing or two about trapping rabbits from those trips with Cecil and even showed the guide a better way of doing it. Each morning we would be woken by the sound of a trumpet playing the 'Morning Reveille', and after breakfast we would be taken on long hikes. No doubt this taste of the bracing life outdoors was designed to prepare us boys for careers in the army. With our experience of the hazards and trials of living outside and our acceptance of discipline and bullying without complaint, we were ideal candidates to take the king's shilling.

Boys will be boys, though, and we did get up to some mischief during those summer camps, particularly after discipline had been relaxed. During one camp at the Duke of Bedford's estate at Woburn Abbey we were all going through puberty and couldn't help looking at the girls and the ways their bodies were changing. There was this large old oak tree on the edge of the secluded area where the girls did their showering, and several of my schoolmates who knew of my climbing prowess egged me on to have a go. A couple of the boughs passed over the wooded area and one was perfect for the job. Though high, it brought me directly above the chattering girls.

I hadn't seen a girl without any clothes on since those baths in the infants' quarters and the changes were astonishing. Although we had all noticed the burgeoning bumps under their school uniforms, it was something else to see them revealed. Yet what shocked me most was how hairy the girls had become. We boys were the same age but had only just started to sprout. I remember sitting astride that bough peering through the leaves and trembling at the excitement of it all.

It had not been an easy climb, and along that thick, stretching bough there was absolutely nothing to hold on to, no twigs or smaller branches, not even a lumpy bit of bark. And it was high. I would probably have broken my neck had I fallen – which might have been the better option than facing the rage of the girls had I dropped into their midst. They would have been mortified to know that I'd seen their exposed bodies and I'm sure they would have never been able to look me in the eye after that.

When I'd managed to edge back along the bough to safety, I had a gaggle of excited boys to report back to. They helped me down and slapped my back – I was clearly the hero of the hour. I didn't spare any detail in my long and lurid account of what I'd seen. Even the girls' leader, Miss Savage, wasn't safe from my pervy eye. She was a very slim pencil-shaped woman and once, years before, her knickers had fallen down while she stretched to write on the blackboard. It was all anyone had talked about for days and now I was finally able to tell the boys what lay beneath those cream bloomers.

When we got back to the Hospital, the boys were keen to see if what I'd told them about the girls was true. It wasn't as if we could just storm into their bathroom, or even casually catch a glimpse through a door left slightly ajar, because we were never allowed near their quarters, nor they near ours; but our dormitories were on the same level, albeit far away on the other side of the school. One boy had the bright idea that we could climb out of the windows in our room and then up the corners of the building to the roof, from which we could edge our way towards the girls' wing. The architecture of the Hospital was Georgian in style, so it had ornate cornicing at every right-angled corner. This cornicing was just deep enough to allow the toes of smallish feet such as ours to get a toehold. We dug our fingers into the stonework and, like the Barbary apes of Gibraltar, inched our way up towards the roof. We moved gingerly and very slowly, and even I, a seasoned climber with a head for heights, made a point of not looking down.

It was a fraught and scary climb, totally reckless, of course, but the reward was sufficient. Once we'd got to the top we were in a much safer position and could scamper across the roof tiles towards the girls' side of the building. There, covered by the darkness of night, we peered into the brightly lit, uncurtained dorms. In truth we didn't see all that much, certainly not enough to warrant taking such a great risk, but we did get a thrill out of seeing the girls in their night clothes talking to each other and getting ready for bed. Their world seemed different to ours – softer and warmer – and I wished ours could be more like theirs.

*

It wasn't long before my attention was grabbed by one girl in particular. Anne arrived with the Berkhamsted children and was eighteen months older than me. She had a good figure and the most stunningly beautiful face. Every boy in the school had a crush on her, and as a result she was never without a beau. Part of her appeal was that she came from the outside world. She had a mother and father and lived in a house – it seemed almost exotic to us.

My first opportunity to get to know her better came when we were paired up for a dancing lesson. It was all very exciting and I couldn't believe I was actually allowed to touch her, but I wasn't a very good dancer, and as I worried about my feet and tried to remember the steps, I could feel my hands getting sweatier and sweatier. I really didn't want to show myself up in front of the girl I fancied. It was excruciating, but I stumbled my way through the waltz and managed the military two-step a little bit better, as it played to our strengths – marching in straight lines with straight legs.

Quite how I managed to collar Anne remains a mystery to me, and I never once felt safe in my ability to keep her. The age gap didn't help: at that stage in my adolescence, those eighteen months seemed like an eternity. And she was so pretty; it was all too good to be true. It really made me feel like the alpha male when she agreed to go out with me.

This is how it happened. At some point in the run-up

to Anne's last Christmas at the school, I found my courage and told her that I liked her. She had ditched her boyfriend a little while before so at least I knew my timing was good. There was some sort of festive soirée at her local parish hall and she managed to get me a ticket. When everyone started playing a game called 'Postman's Knock' – where one person plays the postman and gets a kiss from all the people on his rounds – Anne and I vanished into a darkened area unseen by prying eyes. There I had my first kiss – a 'smackaroo' as we used to call them. Anne was by then fifteen to my thirteen. I don't recall the earth moving or anything like that, but I do remember worrying about what I was doing and whether Anne thought I was as good a kisser as all the others who had had that pleasure before me. I can't have been too bad as she let me hold her hand when we rejoined the game.

Back at school, my status as the new boyfriend of Anne, the hottest and loveliest girl in the school, was confirmed when she chose to spend every break with me. Sadly it didn't last. A few months after we'd started going out, the time came for her to leave and join the world of work. I had a year still to go and once she'd got a job with a company that measured TV ratings I could sense her cooling towards me. I'm sure she thought it was a bit demeaning to be seen going out with a schoolboy. I missed seeing her every day, but I don't think she missed me at all. She was among new people and had money in her pocket and a busy social life. I tried to continue seeing her but there was always some activity or other she was committed to attending.

My life at the Hospital felt empty without her, and having experienced what it was like to have someone, I didn't want to let her go and return to being alone. I'd never had such powerful and intense feelings before and they seemed far more than the natural pangs of first love to me. I didn't know how I was supposed survive without her. She clearly had none of the feelings I had for her. She never told me outright that she wasn't interested in me any more, but I knew this was the case, and I felt angry and upset as if I was just the latest of her many conquests, to be cast aside when she'd had enough.

In the agony of her ebbing interest in me, I became something of a stalker. I used to trek all the way to her village just to catch sight of her and see what she was up to. I took great pains to make sure she didn't see me hiding behind trees and hedges outside her house and ducking into shops when she was walking by: I knew what I was doing wasn't right and I didn't want her to see what a pathetic creature I had become. We had never got any further than kissing – the thought of other things had never even entered my head – but I felt a serious attachment to her that wouldn't go away.

From leaving the Hospital at the age of fifteen, right up to the time I was twenty, I didn't have another girlfriend.

The worries and pressures of staying in work and keeping body and soul together made it a low priority for me, and I didn't have much money, which can't have helped, but the main reason was that I didn't feel able to trust anyone. Anne had betrayed my feelings, she'd hurt me – and I didn't need more of that while I was struggling to survive in the outside world. I felt there was too little of me to give to anyone during that time, and the thought of sharing my troubles and relying on another seemed like an easy way to get my heart broken all over again.

27

Jean

Will It Be Never?

IT SEEMED LIKE A LONG TIME since I'd refused to sign
the adoption papers and I found my guilt increasing every
day. I didn't want to deprive Derek of a happy home life,
but we were still living in Dingwall and I knew that beside
his English accent making him stick out like a sore thumb,
no one would believe he'd been away at boarding school
or any such lie, given that we had been living there for
several years by then.

The only answer was the big city, where we would be
one family among thousands, and this would lend us a
certain amount of anonymity. All we had to do was set
ourselves up with a house and then I would be able to
petition the Hospital to let Derek join us. My husband
didn't take much persuading. I know he loved the Highlands
and would always think of them as home, but the fact of
the matter was that he loved me more and he was

determined to keep the promise he had made before we got married – to help me recover my son.

It took Duncan longer to find a position than I thought it would and I became increasingly impatient as I was worried that time was running out, but eventually, after months of searching, he found a post with a well-established firm in Edinburgh, MacAndrew Wright & Murray, just a few hundred metres from Princes Street, one of the main thoroughfares in the centre. I decided to go back to my old job as a legal secretary with the firm Ketchen & Stevens, only a short distance from my husband's practice. My children were a little older now and I thought the timing was right to make a break with domesticity.

We were living in council accommodation, which wasn't an unusual arrangement for professional people in Scotland in those days. The house was newly built and situated on the outskirts of the city, with beautiful views overlooking the Pentland Hills. There was a problem, however, in that the Foundling Hospital required a mother not only to be married and settled, but also to be able to provide sufficient accommodation for her child, and the housing authority in Edinburgh was only prepared to offer a house adequate to meet the needs of my existing family. I couldn't think how to explain that I wanted a larger one. In an age where there was still so much stigma attached to illegitimacy, how could I – the wife of a professional man – tell a complete stranger that I was a fallen woman and was seeking to gain custody of a child I had given up many years before? I would bring shame on my husband, and I owed it to him to avoid that at all costs.

Once again it seemed that society's rulebook could not easily be broken, and so we began the long process of saving for a deposit to buy our own house. This was something we had been unsuccessfully trying to do for years. It had turned out, to my dismay, that Duncan, had debts when we married. He had never been good with money, and he didn't improve, which put a heavy strain on our relationship at times. When, after only a few months at his new firm, Duncan was offered a partnership, I was over the moon – it was a brilliant opportunity, and he was certainly earning a higher salary, but I just couldn't understand where the money was going. Had he not been such a good and caring husband in every other way, I might have suspected that he was maintaining another woman somewhere. I tried to tackle him about it but he never admitted to a gambling habit or other vice, and I had to conclude that his debts had simply spiralled out of control, to the point where paying off the interest each month became a heavy burden.

As our rows over money escalated, I found myself at a loss as to know what to do. Time was slipping away and my boy was growing up without me. I asked myself again and again if I'd been selfish in not allowing the adoption to go ahead. I had condemned my boy to years more of institutional life when he could have been enjoying the warmth, even love, of a family. I thought about what might happen if by some miracle I was ever able to get in contact. Would he reject my overtures? Would he believe me when I said that I had been trying to get him back for all these years? That I hadn't really wanted to give him up in the first place? There was a good chance that he would hate me for ruining his only prospect of happiness as well as his childhood – and I found this a very hard cross to bear.

One day, my eight-year-old daughter, Katherine, the elder of my two children by Duncan, came home from school in a state of high dudgeon. She complained of bullying from a girl in her class. 'I hate that Sally Divers!' she screamed at me, blurting out the details of what had taken place.

Of course my ears instantly pricked up at the mention of 'Divers'. It was such an unusual name, and even though I hadn't heard from Raymond in fifteen years – for all I knew he had been one of the many fallen in the war – I couldn't help but think that this girl must have some sort of family connection to the man I had once loved. I listened patiently to my daughter's tale before promising to take the matter up with her teacher. 'But first,' I said to my daughter, 'do you think you can find out the full name of Sally's father? I will need that to talk to the teacher.'

It was a calculated move and I wasn't proud of using my

daughter for what was, after all, the longest of long shots. But there was indeed a connection. Little Sally Divers was Raymond's daughter. By the most incredible of coincidences, my daughter and his were classmates, though sadly at daggers drawn. I was glad that he was alive and had escaped the war without injury, although I did suffer a bittersweet pang to learn that he'd moved on and was happy.

Meanwhile the stand-off with the housing authority continued. Unable to persuade them to grant me a larger house and unable to gather enough for a deposit, I began to despair of ever being reunited with my son. Months turned into years and I slowly, finally accepted that my dreams were going to come to nothing. The sense of loss was crushing and this led to an ingrained sadness that I'd never felt before. All through the years, whenever one of my children had a birthday, I would think of Derek and how I could never help him celebrate. On 14 May every year I would do something special – bake a cake, say a prayer or light a candle – just something to mark the occasion. I *never* let it pass unmarked. It was such a beautiful time of year, full of sunshine, blossom and birdsong, but for me its beauty would be forever sullied by the memory of losing my child: the child whom, it now seemed, I would never know.

28

Tom

Into the Unknown

THE LAST FEW MONTHS leading up to August 1954, when I was due to begin my working life, had a surreal quality about them. All the dormitories bar one on the boys' side and one on the girls' were empty now; there were so few of us left that you could wander the corridors from the dorm to hall and then class without meeting another soul. At night-time it was eerily silent. It seemed almost ghostly.

I knew very little of the world beyond the Hospital gates and I wondered how I was ever going to function in it. With no academic qualifications or practical skills, I worried about how I would find a job and a place in society. When I thought about all the years stretching ahead, I felt really scared. It wasn't just the job – it was the whole experience of adult life. I was fifteen and had spent a large part of my life around other children. How was I supposed to know what being an adult required? I still liked playing games like British Bulldog and singing silly rhymes to the girls and seeing how many gobstoppers I could fit into my mouth at once. These were childish practices and they would have to stop.

It was a bright early summer's day – just like the day on which I had arrived at the Foundling Hospital – when I finally turned my back on the awe-inspiring building and passed through those grand iron gates for the last time. I was sad to be leaving. The first few years there had been miserable, true, but the Hospital had always shielded me from the outside world. It had become my home, and over the years life there had improved beyond recognition. I was old enough to understand why I had been put there and that being 'illegitimate' had left a mark on me. I was also aware that we'd all been cocooned from any censure or discrimination. Would it be different from now on? We'd heard of foundlings getting the sack when their employers discovered their origins and my head was whirring with questions: Would people treat me badly if they found out about my birth? Would they trust me? What if they tarnished me with the same brush that my mother surely had been?

But there was no holding back time. Armed with a personalized Holy Bible, a new suit and a new pair of shoes, I stepped into a world for which I was woefully underprepared and from which I had been isolated for ten years. I was lucky – my foster parents, George and Bessie, were there to welcome me, and I went to live with them permanently.

At first everything seemed to be going well – it was like an extended summer holiday. I helped George in the garden and Bessie set me to work around the house on my very first day.

'Let's get these old carpets outside and on the line, shall we?' She picked up a small rug and I collected the others, lugging them out through the door and into the garden. I hung a couple on the cord that served as a washing line and we started beating them with paddles to get the dust and dirt out.

'Deary me, I'm not sure I can stand this,' Bessie said, coughing and spluttering as a thick cloud of dust enveloped her. 'I've been meaning to do this for such a long time but I just don't seem to have the strength in my arms any more.'

She was in her late sixties by then and increasingly frail. I didn't like to see her downcast, so I smiled and said, 'You're as strong as ever, Ma. It's just that I'm stronger!' I whacked the carpets as hard as I could to prove my point.

'Get away with you,' she said affectionately and left me to it.

Bessie was really happy to have me there and made a celebratory lunch of roast pork with crackling and apple sauce made from George's Bramleys. The meal was delicious, and, even better, I got to spread the dripping onto some bread for my supper. I used to love skewering the bread with an iron fork and toasting it over the fire in winter, or the gas hob in summer, before slathering on the dripping. Bessie's was rich, flavoured with salt and had the consistency of butter – it was a real delicacy and so much better than the grease the Hospital used to serve up several times a week.

We had a good chat about work that evening, and I was pleased to find out that George and Bessie had managed to get me a job with their friend, Nick Straighton, who was an optician and owned a couple of shops in the area. We had visited his posh house in the seaside town of Hove, about fifty miles from the shop in Feltham, a few times. I was always curious about George's and his relationship – the well-to-do businessman and the humble railway guard. For some reason they got on really well, though George would fawn over Nick whenever they met – complimenting him on his swish new suit or expensive greenhouse – and I would squirm with embarrassment because I thought it was demeaning. Bessie didn't make such a show of herself and could always hold her own in conversation. I was always proud to see her in action, arguing the political questions of the day with such an intelligent businessman.

In those days, opticians often doubled as photographic retail shops and portrait studios, so I knew that the job wouldn't be dull, even if I was just operating the till. As is happened, I was taken on as the photographer's assistant and set about learning the art of professional photography, which included portraiture, weddings, events and then processing the images in the darkroom. It was interesting work and I counted myself very lucky. I couldn't have wished for a better start. I was so fired up that I enrolled for evening classes in photography and looked forward to gaining my first qualifications. For the first time I saw a future opening up in front of me.

I enjoyed the job and found the process of developing photographs fascinating. From a plain white sheet of paper an image would appear, as if by magic. I learned how to use chemicals to develop negatives, and although it was an exciting process, it was also a little scary because you never got a second chance; if you messed up, that was it. I particularly liked a piece of equipment called 'the enlarger', which increased the size of the images, sometimes to fit huge frames. It looked a bit like a giant microscope and I felt like a scientist when I adjusted the lenses. The darkroom was spooky at first but I grew to love the infrared light and peculiar vinegar-like smell. While I was in there I didn't have to think about anything other than the image appearing before me. It required calm concentration – something I didn't mind at all after the hustle and bustle of the Hospital.

It was a great, though worrying, moment for me when several months into my traineeship I was judged to have made sufficient progress to be trusted with a wedding. I was always taking pictures in my spare time and my boss had been impressed with my compositions and use of light. He said I was a natural, with a photographer's eye. But it does seem odd, reflecting on it now. What must the guests have thought of the fresh-faced youth who turned up to record for posterity their big day – the day they had spent a small fortune on? It was a big responsibility. Events like that can't be restaged so I only had one chance to get the shots right, and if I didn't capture the right moments – the bride looking beautiful, the groom looking happy, the bride's father looking proud, the cutting of the cake, the couple gazing lovingly into each other's eyes – I would ruin their memories for all time.

Stress threatened to overwhelm me all day long. I could even feel my hands shaking on the shutter. I just didn't know how I would face my boss – or worse, the newly-weds – if I messed up. It would be a sacking offence, for sure.

Luckily the guests seemed to listen to my directions. I was in a smart suit, which may have given me a little gravitas, and I was fairly tall, so perhaps I looked older than my years. And I knew that I came across as a rather serious boy in those days. Bessie had said as much the night before when she'd noticed I was uncharacteristically quiet and asked me what was up.

'You'll manage it, Tommy. If you apply yourself tomorrow, it'll be all right. Don't you worry; they'll do exactly what you tell them to do. Just don't be shy!' she said, before making me some warm milk with Horlicks. In her world this solved virtually every problem, big· or small.

I took her pep talk to heart and clung on to an air of quiet professionalism as I shepherded everyone into place and asked them to look this way and then that – and to smile. Why people wouldn't smile at a wedding is beyond me but some of the guests certainly needed chivvying a bit. It was a eureka moment when I rushed back to the darkroom to process the film and I saw the images coming up sharp and clear with plenty of contrast. *Phew!* I thought to myself. *Maybe I can do this after all.*

A less stressful part of the job was portrait photography. It was more intimate and you knew you could do a retake. I found the whole business a little stilted and staged, though. People seemed to adopt faces – a grin to look happy, a pout to look sexy and a slight frown to look serious – hoping these would impress the viewer, but all these expressions seemed phoney to me and utterly untrue to the person's real character.

My employer told me at the start that it was very important to feed people's egos and tell them what a charming or handsome couple they made or what beautiful children they had.

'Flattery is the thing,' he insisted after seeing me smirk when he praised one lady's 'luscious lips'. She was a big woman with rolls of fat that wobbled as she walked. No part of her looked luscious to me.

'But sir,' I said, 'she's not much of a looker, is she? Surely she knows that.'

'Trust me, Tom,' he replied. 'People like to hear good things about themselves, even if they know they're not strictly true. They'll be putty in your hands, my boy, if you flatter them enough.'

He was right. Everyone wanted to feel like a model or a film star – and I would always be rewarded with a brilliant smile if my compliment hit the spot. I found it unsettling at first. I'd spent ten years in an institution where we all looked and dressed the same; there were no mirrors and no one ever told us we looked nice. I was not used to giving or receiving praise – and I couldn't understand how people could fall for it.

One part of the job that I found really difficult was taking portraits of children. Whether they were happy and smiling or stroppy and crying, it was clear that all the little kids who came through our doors were loved. I remember thinking how strong the bonds between parents and their children were and how much I would have liked some of that closeness myself. There was one family that upset me so much I had to go to the darkroom afterwards to compose myself. The mother was young and pretty and wore this full blue skirt with little white flowers that swirled around her as she moved. She removed her tiny white gloves to reveal the most delicate hands you could imagine, and then, licking a couple fingers, she proceeded to wipe a dirty mark off her son's cheek. A plump little chap, he was dressed in a blue and white sailor's uniform – which I think is why the scene had such an effect on me. The father stood with an arm around his wife while she held the baby aloft, and then they looked adoringly into each other's eyes and I took the shot. It was perfect. This, I told myself, is the life I could have had with a family who loved me.

Around this time my relationship with my foster parents began to sour. I was grateful for their help in getting me such an interesting job and I had enjoyed my school holidays at their house, but I was finding it difficult to get along with them now we were together all the time. As the months went by, we began to argue more and more. Part of the problem was that they were so old and so stuck in their ways. They still saw me as a child and didn't want to give me any independence, which meant they wanted me home by nine-thirty every night, even at the weekends, so while other boys my age were allowed to go out to dances and youth clubs, I had to sit around with a couple old enough to be my grandparents. When I asked for my own key so I could come and go without bothering them all the time, they refused, which made me think that they hadn't really accepted me as a member of the family. I started to feel more like a lodger than their son. All my friends had keys – and I pointed this out to my foster parents – but they wouldn't budge. I can see now that it must have been difficult for them too. I was no longer the cute, if troublesome, little boy they had once wanted to adopt, but a testosterone-fuelled youth who argued with them round the clock. But I couldn't see that then.

I tried to distract myself from the tension at home by writing to my "girlfriend" Anne. She replied a couple of times but her letters were always short and she never answered my suggestion that we should meet up. I realized then that those last few embers had definitely gone out. If I couldn't maintain her interest when I was still in her neighbourhood, I was never going to do it from forty miles away. Looking back, I was pretty cut up about the whole affair. And seeing me so glum and mopey probably added to George and Bessie's annoyance.

I did have an ally – Bessie's kindly spinster cousin, May, or Aunt May, as I used to call her. She came to stay every weekend, travelling the few miles from Kingston upon Thames where she spent the week in digs while she was working in a department store called Bentalls. You could set your watch by her arrival. She caught exactly the same train every weekend and took the same amount of time to walk from the station to our house. She was such a creature of habit; maybe that's why she kept coming. Bessie wasn't very nice to her so I couldn't understand it otherwise.

May was in her late fifties – ten years younger than Bessie

– and she didn't seem to have one grey strand in her jet-black hair. If I met her now, I would think that she dyed it, but dyes weren't common in those days. She was amazingly short, not standing even as high as five feet, and she had allowed herself to become dumpy, unlike her lean cousin. I bet she was pretty when she was younger, but by the time I knew her she kind of waddled. She was kind to me, though, and would bring me things from the store – sweets, or a new pair of socks, or a game we could play together. Bessie always seemed to disapprove and would tell May off for spoiling my dinner or exciting me before bedtime. I suspect now that she was jealous. She could be quite possessive at times and I don't think she liked May to get too close.

May's early story is a sad one. Her mother died when she was around eight years old and she was cared for by her womanizing, drink-loving father. He couldn't cope, and in the end her mum's sister – Bessie's mum – took her in. She was a waif at this point, undernourished and wearing tatty clothes – 'a dirty little urchin', as Bessie once said unkindly. Although they were the only children in the house, there were ten years between them and they never played together. I suspect Bessie came to regard May as a cuckoo in the nest for stealing her mother's attention away from her. She always seemed to want to put May in her place. 'Where would you have been if it weren't for my parents?' she used to say if May ever spoke about her job or about buying a new pair of shoes.

In fact Bessie was positively cruel to May at times. She'd make jibes about her weight or rub in the fact that her father was a 'no-good drunk'. Bessie was a bit of a snob in her way. She never stopped rubbing it in that she had been a music teacher while May had gone into service, that she owned her own house while May lived in digs, that she was from a middle-class teetotal family while May was from a troubled one. She loved raking over old coals and drawing comparisons. May was very much the 'below stairs' member of the family and she was not allowed to forget it.

'Look how your father used to show mine up by letting you stay off school,' she said once. 'And my dad, a school attendance officer. Do you know how embarrassing it was that someone in his own family was too drunk to get up in the morning and get his child off to school? Well, do you? And when you did get there, do you remember the state you were in? Grotty clothes and a dirty face . . . We were all mortified. I'm not saying it was your fault, May,' Bessie finally conceded, 'but you don't know how it humiliated my family.'

May always looked wretched at this. She never answered back or tried to defend herself. Perhaps she was so used to putting up with Bessie's haranguing that she considered it par for the course. I felt so sorry for her, especially when George, usually such an inoffensive man, chipped in with his pennyworth, no doubt feeling that it was his duty to support his wife in this as in all things. The worst of it was that they'd go on and on about her wanting to inherit the house after they'd gone. As far as I could see, this wasn't true at all. Why would she be so nice to me if she wanted their money? Surely I would have represented a threat?

It did make me wonder, though, why she put up with it all. I don't think Aunt May was after an inheritance, but she wasn't very well off so security could have played a part. Perhaps she couldn't afford to stay in digs over the weekend. Or perhaps she was just clinging to the only family she'd ever known. I felt we shared a bond, Aunt May and I. We were kindred spirits, both having struggled through difficult childhoods, both considered among life's losers. George and Bessie expected us to be so grateful to them – and indeed I was grateful, but I didn't want to be reminded of it all the time. I just wanted to forget what had gone before and make a new life.

The rows became more and more heated until a point was reached where George and Bessie had had enough.

'Your mother, if she was here, might have put up with this, Tommy, but we're not your real parents and we can't go on,' Bessie said, wringing her hands, after one argument. 'You're going to have to leave.'

I don't blame them really. They were both pensioners and should have been putting their feet up and relaxing into their retirement by this time, rather than dealing with a stroppy, troubled youth. The generation gap that lay between us was too great. They had no real experience of children and I didn't have any of home life. It was a lesson in the dangers of institutionalizing young people. There was no going back and no meeting in the middle. I had been given my marching orders, and that was it, the end of my childhood.

I ended up in St George's Hostel for boys in Brixton, London. It was a grim place with more than its share of misfits, and from the outside it looked like an old Victorian workhouse. My heart sank when I saw the broken windows and cold stone floors and the grotty room I would be expected to share with three other young men, but it was all I could afford. I began almost immediately to regret that I hadn't made a bigger effort with my foster parents. Still, it was a long way from the shock I had experienced when I'd arrived at the Foundling Hospital. Few things could ever be as terrifying as that.

My accommodation was a long way from the optician's shop in Feltham. I faced a round trip of twenty-six miles each day, but I was never late – not once. Yet, to my dismay, my boss took a very dim view of the fact that I had failed to make the grade with my foster parents and suggested I should seek alternative work closer to where I lived. Effectively, it was the sack.

That job was the only good thing in my life. It had kept me going through all the disagreements at home and without it I was at a dead end. Not only had I enjoyed it but I'd worked really hard. I was a good employee: never late, always polite and my pictures were starting to look really good. It was another rejection – one that I didn't understand or deserve – and I was furious at the injustice.

One cold November night I travelled to the shop and climbed in through the roof skylight, dropping down to the floor below. I had decided to take what I thought was owed to me – a camera, some lenses and a few other bits of kit that were necessary to the would-be freelance photographer. It didn't seem like breaking the law, not really. My boss had committed the first wrong in sacking me and I was read-dressing the balance. Besides, I needed these things to survive. I knew the place like the back of my hand and didn't think anything could go wrong. But I guess I wasn't thinking clearly because I was stupid enough to turn on an internal light.

Policing in those days was a much more 'boots on the ground' affair. It was normal police procedure to check that shop doors were securely locked and that nothing looked amiss inside. Unfortunately for me, a beady-eyed policeman noticed the light deep within the shop and raised the alarm.

When I saw the beam of his torch on me, I quickly made my escape through the same skylight. Meanwhile the policeman ran round the side of the building and I found myself being chased through the rain into an industrial estate. Younger, fitter and fleeter of foot than my pursuer, I managed to get away, but it was late and the last train to London had already left. There was nothing to do but hide the equipment and wander the rainy streets until morning. Inevitably a patrol car came across me and, tired, wet and dispirited, I allowed myself to be taken into custody.

The following day I appeared in court. I felt sick as they read out the charge of 'breaking and entering' – a serious offence which could land me with a stint in a borstal young offenders' institute. I pleaded guilty and couldn't believe I was in such a mess. Sixteen years old and my fingerprints had joined those of the criminal fraternity. To make matters worse, Feltham, the most notorious borstal in the country, lay close by in the very jurisdiction of the court that was to try me. I'd only just left one gated institution, and now I was headed for another – by all accounts, an even worse one. Labour, routine, discipline, authority: these were to be the cornerstones of my life, it seemed.

It was the last thing I was expecting, but just in the nick of time two representatives from the Foundling Hospital arrived to save me. They swooped in from the London office, much like the cavalry coming over the top of the hill, and after a few quiet words with the magistrate, during which it was established that they were acting in *loco parentis* and could vouch for my character and the difficulties I had been through lately, I was free to go. The court was prepared to be lenient and would release me on the condition that I told the police where the loot was stashed.

That was the end of the matter, except that I now had a criminal record.

29

Tom

A Time of Decision

Iᴛ ᴡᴀꜱ ᴍɪᴅ-ᴡɪɴᴛᴇʀ, 1955. I was sixteen and living in an antiquated hostel without proper heating. I had no money, and with no job or qualifications my situation began to look very bleak. At least the country was slowly getting back on its feet after the desperate years following the war. The transport and construction industries were picking up, houses were being built, and there were jobs out there, but as I had a criminal record and no permanent address, things didn't look good. Apprenticeships were the best way to learn a trade or skill, but these were often arranged by one's parents. I didn't see how I could get one without someone paying the owner of the business the sum required to take me on and teach me the ropes. I had burned my bridges with George and Bessie and there was no one else I could ask. It wasn't like it is now – unemployment benefit for school leavers didn't exist. In order to live, I had to find a job. There was no other option.

I still desperately wanted to continue in photography and was thrilled when the Foundling Hospital offered to buy me some equipment. Rather than give me the money directly, they instructed me to choose a camera and a few other bits of apparatus and then forward the bills for them to pay. It was great being able to take pictures again but I didn't have the confidence or experience to set myself up as a freelance photographer, and I decided the best course of action would be to find employment in the field and keep practising in my spare time. With this in mind, I began to cold-call press agencies, newspapers and camera shops until I found someone willing to take me on. My persistence paid off and I managed to find myself a job as a runner in a Fleet Street photographic news agency called Paul Popper Ltd. This involved delivering news photographs from home and abroad direct to the art editors of the various newspapers and magazines based in the capital. Reading the captions and perusing the pictures, the editors would decide if they were interested. It was interesting work and it gave me a great buzz to walk through the doors of all the leading newspapers and periodicals of the day.

The boss of the firm, a Czech-born Jew called Paul Popper, had emigrated to London in the early 1930s when the climate turned against Jews and made it difficult for him to go on living and working as a journalist on the continent. He had used his connections with European photographers to establish the agency and continued to write features and take photographs himself. I wonder whether he saw something of his younger self in me – a rootless youth who was desperate to make something of himself despite growing up in adversity. I had given the Hospital as a reference, and I'm sure they must have told him all about my troubled background; it's possible this was part of the reason why he gave me the job. Although it paid poorly and involved working Monday to Saturday, Paul was always very considerate towards me. Charity was an important part of his religion and he would give me items of clothing for which he had no further use: expensive silk ties, socks and shirts came my way, all of which I could not possibly have afforded myself.

After a while, it seemed to me that Paul looked on himself as something of a father figure to me. This had its limits, however, as I found out one day. While in the Golders Green area of London, home to a large and illustrious Jewish community, I decided to call at his house and say hello. I met with a distinctly frosty reception. 'What are you doing here?' he enquired without a trace of warmth. Instead of being asked in for a cup of tea, as I had expected, I was sent on my way with a flea in my ear and told not to come back again. Perhaps he knew about the break-in and didn't want to take any chances. Or perhaps he simply didn't feel as close to me as I did to him. Either way, the rejection and humiliation were intense.

For the two years I continued to work at the agency, I never tried to get close to him again, which was difficult to begin with as I felt very alone in the world. The hostel was five miles south of Fleet Street, and with money so tight, walking there and back was often my only option. Sometimes I took to riding the underground without paying, and was caught twice and hauled back into court. I was fined on both occasions, which annoyed me, but I wasn't overly upset by the experience. There was no one in my life to disappoint, no one to care that I'd let myself down again. Eventually I teamed up with a friend from the Foundling Hospital, Fred Jacks, and together we were just about able to pay the rent on a small flat. I was glad to escape the hostel, but I felt restless. Being a courier didn't allow me to develop my photographic or journalistic skills, or, better still, type the captions that accompanied each photo before it went to the art editor, and this had begun to depress me.

It seemed to me that there must be more to life than I had experienced at the Hospital or in my daily couriering job. I was seventeen and really bored with my work. I didn't have a girlfriend or many friends, and I badly needed a change of scenery.

One morning I decided it was time to take a break from the city. London was beginning to get me down. I would brighten up my life by taking a cycling holiday in France.

I could pedal the six hundred miles from St Malo to the Spanish holiday resort of San Sebastian and back again. And I would do it all in a fortnight. It was an extraordinarily ambitious undertaking – one most people would have regarded as plain foolhardy – but I had set my mind to do it and so I would. Fred agreed to come too. However, he backed out with some lame excuse at the eleventh hour. He'd probably got a rush of common sense. Faced with cancelling my much-looked-forward-to holiday or sallying forth alone, I opted for the latter.

I was used to cycling the sixty miles from London to a south coast resort on Sundays, spending a few hours at the beach, and then cycling back again before dark. I was young, fit and healthy, so it seemed like there was nothing to it. But this was a challenge of a wholly different order. Laden down with a tent, cooking utensils and supplies, I caught the early ferry from Portsmouth and arrived in northern France eager to start my adventure. By the time I'd battled across the torturous gradients of Brittany all the way to Nantes, it was dusk. There, exhausted and a little downcast, I parked my bike against the kerb. It was so heavy with the saddlebag and panniers that the moment I let go of the handlebars, the front wheel shot up into the air and I had to grab the frame quickly to stop it from falling. From then on I had to lay the bike on its side whenever I stopped for a break.

The first hundred miles of the journey had been so

arduous that when I looked at the map the following morning and saw hundreds more remaining, I decided to cheat a little. I would catch a train for the next two hundred miles to Bordeaux and then give myself a little extra time in San Sebastian, the Spanish resort just across the border. But standing at the train station ticket office, I found myself getting into difficulty. I was trying to explain in hopeless French that I wanted a return for both myself and the bike. The Hospital had never given us any language tuition so I didn't know how on earth to translate 'bicycle'. A sizable queue was building up behind me and I could feel myself getting redder and redder. Only when my difficulties threatened the loss of her train did a young French woman step forward from right behind me and – in perfect English – bring an end to the impasse. I remember burning with indignation. I hated to be made to look stupid, and I felt she had taken perverse pleasure in seeing me make a fool of myself.

For almost a fortnight I didn't speak to anyone in my own language, and since I spoke no other, it was, effectively, a fortnight of silence. I will never forget the endlessly straight flat road that ran through Les Landes forest and stretched for a hundred miles along the Bay of Biscay. It had been designed by Napoleon's engineers to stabilize the shallow topsoil and was an impressive sight. For a day and a half it refused to yield to my ceaseless pedalling. As flat as a pancake, the landscape never seemed to change, and half an hour could elapse before a car went by. I was left alone with my thoughts for much of the day. When darkness fell, I would pitch my tent a few yards into the forest or sneak into a farmer's barn, if I could see one, and find some hay on which to spend the night.

It was, without doubt, a strange and solitary holiday. I still look back on it as a huge achievement. It certainly marked me out as an eccentric at work, though. They couldn't believe that I had cycled six hundred miles alone for no other reason than that I thought it a good idea. I was naïve and idealistic in so many ways. I didn't see obstacles – only hurdles to jump over.

While my sheltered life had made me something of a dreamer, it had also made me rather easy to shock. On the ferry back to England, I met a French couple who were also planning to cycle home to London. It was lovely to chat after so many days of silence, and they turned out to be a really interesting pair; the wife had been secretary to General de Gaulle during his wartime exile in Britain. We decided to make the sixty-mile journey together. Halfway along the route, on an open stretch of straight road, the ex-secretary called a halt. She needed to relieve herself. Dismounting, she stepped back from the kerb a couple of paces, hoisted her skirt to her waist, pulled down her panties to her knees and went into a squat position. Then she proceeded, in full view of the passing traffic, to have a torrential pee.

Recounting this story on my first day back at work, I

was surprised to learn that this was not the least unusual for a French person – man or woman – at that time. Years later I observed a man brazenly having a pee against the front wall of the Louvre. Even now I can't imagine how people would react if this were to happen against the brickwork of the Tate Modern.

Although I went back to my press agency job after my holiday, little by little I lost interest in it. I began to feel like a general dogsbody. I was not only couriering images but also fetching and carrying personal items for Paul. He'd send me all over London to pick up books, new clothes and his favourite coffee beans – and I was getting tired of it. Slowly my thoughts turned in another direction. I was coming up to eighteen, and it wasn't long before I could expect my call-up papers to do my two years of National Service with the military. Rather than wait it out, I decided to apply for early enlistment.

30

Tom

Army Days

For most young men, National Service was an unpleasant interruption to normal life and many would seek to put it off as long as possible. But for me, fed up and seemingly going nowhere, a return to institutional life actually had its own appeal. I wanted to belong to a group again, and to feel that I was being challenged and achieving something. There was certainly no institution more challenging than the army.

In the early autumn of 1957, I reported for six weeks' basic training with the 11th Hussars at Carlisle near the Scottish border. Nicknamed 'the Cherry Pickers', the 11th Hussars had gained their unusual nickname because in the heat of a particularly fierce Napoleonic battle, when their services were urgently required to stave off defeat, they were finally run to ground in a cherry orchard nonchalantly doing what soldiers do: living off the land. Given my past disaster with cherries, I'm not sure it was a good omen.

My destination was Hadrian's camp, located at the western end of the famous wall, where the 11th Hussars were serving their turn as the training regiment for the cavalry corps. The cavalry still maintained a number of horses, used largely for ceremonial duties, since armoured vehicles were used in battle now. National Service recruits from the regiment had just returned from combat operations in the Malayan Emergency and had also helped to diffuse tensions in Oman. Britain had withdrawn from Egypt after the Suez fiasco, but it was still the dominant power in the Middle East and had responsibilities extending throughout the now crumbling Empire. It was still an exciting time for soldiering and there was a real chance I would see action after basic training.

I was one of seventy-five National Service recruits drafted from all over the country and from all backgrounds. Upper-class public schoolboys – even an aristocrat's son – were billeted with the sons of miners. It was an amazing cross-section of the social strata of the day. Unlike the systems that operated in many other countries, wealthy or well-connected fathers couldn't pull any strings to help their sons avoid conscription, and there was absolutely no favouritism shown by those in charge once we were there.

For almost all the intake, those first few days of military life were extremely unpleasant. From the demeaning buzz cut to a series of rapid-fire painful inoculations through to kitting-out and marching all over the place, it never stopped. I saw shock and exhaustion on many faces as the boys took to their beds that first night. I'm sure they were thinking about everyone they'd left behind – the parents who loved them, brothers, sisters, girlfriends, the warm and friendly communities they'd sprung from. There were numerous gruelling exercises and the troop sergeant never ceased screaming obscenities at us throughout. Even normal talk, which seemed rare, was delivered in a raised voice; barked might be the term. For boys who had never been away from home, the camp must have seemed hellish.

It was different for me. I had few fond memories to draw on, and while they were dreaming of home comforts, I thought back to those first few years at the Hospital: the nightmarish bullying of the dormitories, the rigid routine and harsh discipline. Although I was far from happy, I at least knew I could get through it.

My troop sergeant, it turned out, was on a mission, the mission being to gain the coveted sash for the best troop of the three who were undertaking the six weeks' basic training. He was about to leave the army, and having won the two previous sashes, there was no way he was going to allow this 'steaming heap of shit' (as he insisted on calling us) to rob him of his just deserts: a hat trick. He wanted to go out on a high and would brook no performance that put his mission in jeopardy. Humiliation and punishment awaited anyone whose efforts weren't top-drawer.

Basic training consisted of several activities: 'square-bashing' (slang for drill on a barrack's square), rifle-shooting, map-reading, initiative tests and maintaining the standard of our kit. Very early on I received a tip that would serve me in good stead: to perform all my tasks sufficiently well not to be noticed. That way, my name would not trip off the troop sergeant's tongue readily since he would have hardly ever heard it. The word was that once he had screamed at you for your name, you were dead in the water. Thereafter, you could expect to be picked on and singled out for his very special blend of brutal nastiness. Years later, a scene in Stanley Kubrick's film *Full Metal Jacket* reminded me of the kind of verbal diarrhoea we had to put up with. I had had my share of hardship in times past, but dysentery of speech was new to me.

Inevitably, when it came to drill, the troop had its quota of recruits with two left feet. The sergeant's greatest disdain was reserved for the man who, on the command 'left' or 'right turn' would do the opposite. Then all hell would break loose. Screaming at the top of his voice for the twenty-five-man troop to halt, he would demand that the unfortunate miscreant quick-march to where he stood. Then, red-faced, with neck veins bulging and his nose inches from the unfortunate youth's face, he would hurl and spit a torrent of foul-mouthed abuse at him the like of which none of us had ever heard before – or could have thought possible in a single breath. If he was really mad he would tear off his beret, throw it high into the air and jump up and down on it when it landed. I always pitied the recruits who had to face this – they were dead meat.

The cavalry to which the 11th Hussars belonged liked to look down on the infantry, taking the view that he who rode into battle must – by the nature of things – be superior to he who walked. I'm sure this was one of the reasons our sergeant was so stern: he told us that we had to be the best and we had to do the regiment proud. Just like the Foundling Hospital, every regiment and every individual had a place in the hierarchical pecking order. I was under no illusion that I was once again at the bottom of the pyramid.

As in my former life, exercise and cleaning took priority. Reveille was sounded every morning at five-thirty, and by six a.m. we were to be found jogging in our hobnailed boots along the chilly November lanes of Cumbria, close to the Scottish border. Boots were the pride and joy of the 11th Hussars. Other regiments might polish their brasses to a higher sparkle, or another regiment get its creases sharper and so on, but none in the entire army excelled at boot-shine as the 11th Hussars liked to think they did. And what a price the young recruits were expected to pay to maintain the myth.

Night after night we would sit hunched over a candle, boots stuffed tight with damp newspapers until they were solid lumps weighing twice their normal weight. The boots' mottled leather surface would be ironed until it was entirely smooth. That's where the candle came in. We would each heat a spoon over the flame and then use it to smooth and flatten the mottle out of the leather. Then the awesomely tedious process would begin of applying spit, cloth and polish over and over again. My fingers ached unbearably afterwards. Every day these sessions would take place; by the end of the six weeks we must have worked a few millimetres of polish onto the surface. The aim was to bring the boots up to the level of patent leather. Even the black paint on the eyelets would be scraped off to reveal the brass below, and then this would be polished. And the whole agonizing process was leading up to one thing – the passing-out parade.

As this fateful event drew closer, we worked hard to ensure the boots were reaching their final thrilling state of perfection. One day in the final week of training, the troop sergeant strode purposefully into the billet for an inspection of this most prized item of the recruit's kit. It was a freezing day yet, strangely, he ordered that all windows facing the parade ground be opened to their full extent. Then, with baton tight under his armpit, he slowly advanced down the line of beds, sniffing, snorting and making a range of peculiar sounds as he examined each pair of boots. Each recruit stood to attention at the end of his bed. Suddenly he alighted upon a pair which caused him to stiffen and let out a cry like a wounded animal. Then, with eyes bulging, he lifted the offending boot slowly at arm's length with the tip of his baton as though it was smelly rubbish.

Grabbing the boot from the end of his baton he raised it high – uttering a string of the vilest of profanities imaginable – and hurled it straight through the open window onto the barrack square beyond. He repeated the exercise with the other boot. As they bounced and skidded across the tarmac surface, which tore and scratched the glass-like finish of the boots, the unfortunate young recruit clasped both hands to the side of his head and, bending low, let out a wail. With only days to go before the passing-out parade, he knew that he would be up every night until the small hours to make good the damage inflicted. It was a cruel thing for the troop sergeant to have done.

When the day came, we all felt extremely nervous. A general was chauffeured in and took his place on the saluting dais, along with other top brass and various civic dignitaries from Carlisle. This way and then that the three competing troops paraded, one at a time, showing off the full range of the drill they had practised during the preceding six weeks. Finally, manoeuvres complete, all three troops lined up to await the two big decisions of the day: best troop and best recruit. A great cheer went up from my troop as it was declared the winner, before a pregnant hush descended as they awaited the announcement of best recruit.

All three troops, seventy-five men in all, were standing at ease with their hands clasped behind their backs.

Suddenly I felt an elbow from the next trooper jab me. I ignored it and hoped the sergeant hadn't seen. To fall out of line now would be a catastrophe. Everything felt a bit surreal, almost as if I was in another world. It was the relief of having reached this point without messing up any of the demonstration drill manoeuvres – the feeling was so great that I was quite oblivious to those about me. Abruptly, the elbow struck again, breaking my reverie.

'Wake up, you silly sod, it's you . . . it's you!' hissed the trooper under his breath.

I suddenly realized what the jabs were all about. I couldn't believe it – I had won the accolade of best recruit. Snapping to attention, I brought my right knee up high and then smashed it down hard. I took one step back from the line – again with another knee-high flourish and crashing boot – before turning smartly to the right. Then I marched briskly round the three lines of troops and presented myself before the saluting dais. With all the swagger I could muster, I brought my boot down with an almighty thump and saluted the inspecting general with a final flourish. He returned the salute and smiled.

'Well done, soldier,' he said and handed me the coveted award. It was all pure theatre, but it was, nonetheless, the proudest moment of my young life.

For a while afterwards, I remained puzzled at my good fortune. With the exception of the initiative tests, I didn't recall winning any of the other five disciplines, although I knew I'd scored well in all of them. But I worked out that it was the soldier with the highest average score – and it was true, I had performed above average in every discipline. Apart from securing my county colours for swimming when I was thirteen, it was the first time I had won anything in my life.

The parade had been such an important fixture in my mind that when it was all over I felt a huge sense of relief. It was as if a weight had been lifted from my shoulders and I could start to get excited about the next stage in my army life.

British troops were stationed all over the world at that time, but we had been told that we would be posted to one of three locations: fifty recruits were to go to BAOR (the British Army of the Rhine); twenty to Hong Kong; and the remaining five to the army's worst posting, Northern Ireland – the British soldier's Siberia, with rain instead of snow. I thought these were pretty good odds. Hong Kong was my preferred choice, but Germany would do. Some of the older soldiers spoke about the country in quite romantic terms – grand old cities, beautiful landscapes and comely fräuleins, the last of which interested me no end. Statistically I thought I would have to be very unlucky to go to Northern Ireland. But 'Murphy's Law' damned me and I was sent to join the 15th/19th The King's Royal Hussars in the soldier's Siberia.

My arrival at Lisanelly Barracks in Omagh, County Tyrone

was dismal. As if to confirm the wretchedness of my luck, it rained almost ceaselessly for six weeks. But then came a lucky break. As the second most senior officer in the regiment, the auspiciously named Major Hodgson was President of the Regimental Institute, and, as such, was responsible for the organization and accounting of the social side of regimental life. The Major was Second-in-Command and had other more important duties to consider, such as maintaining discipline, instructing junior officers and supervising weapons training, so he used to appoint one of the lower ranks to take charge of the office. The appointment carried an automatic promotion to lance corporal and was seen as a cushy position, as it involved spending more time in the office than outside performing drills. The corporal who was then running the office was coming to the end of his National Service and so the post was about to fall vacant. To my surprise, I found myself nominated for the position.

'Consider yourself a jammy bastard,' the soon-to-be demobbed corporal said to me when I was introduced to him. He set about explaining my new duties. 'For starters, you're answerable, first and foremost, to the Second-in-Command of the Regiment. He's your boss. Your job is the office and to keep it off his back. As such you're excused just about every fricking duty you can think of, including that bastard, Morning Parade.'

'Bloody hell,' I replied, 'that's marvellous!'

After setting out a schedule for me and going over the

various files, he gave me a pat on the back. 'Lucky bastard,' he said again as he took his leave.

Two days later, on a Monday morning, I arrived to take up my new duties. Alone in my new domain, I strutted back and forth like the cock of the roost feeling exceedingly pleased with myself. But there was, nevertheless, an element of apprehension. Would I be up to it? What if I were to disappoint? I sat in my chair and slid open one of the steel cabinet files. Suddenly a series of rapid-fire taps came from the direction of the office windows. Startled, I looked up.

Outside stood an overweight, red-faced lance corporal with ginger hair. 'What the fuck are you doing sitting down there?' he demanded in an abrasive, Ulster brogue. 'Why aren't you up on the fucking square ready for Morning Parade?'

'Because I was told that I was excused,' I replied defensively, a little confused by the ferocity of his approach.

'Well, I'm telling you you're fucking not. Get your fucking arse up there *now*!'

The confrontational tone, laced with what I took to be real malice, began to anger me. I had followed the rules and had done exactly as I had been told. This ruddy upstart had no business telling me what to do.

'Speak to Major Hodgson,' I shot back, 'he's my boss.'

'Are you fucking with me?' the corporal challenged. 'I'm giving you a direct order. Get your fucking arse up on to the square. Now!'

'Piss off!' I replied dismissively. I was incensed by the corporal's attitude and returned to my files.

'Piss off . . . piss off . . . ? Is that what you said? Is that what you said!' screamed the corporal, running round from the window and bursting in through the door.

'Yes, piss off. That *is* exactly what I said, and if you don't, I'll fucking give you a hand!'

The corporal gave a snort. He was incandescent with rage. Then the snort slowly morphed into a triumphant, self-satisfied grin. 'Right, that's all I need,' he said, lowering his voice in a sinister fashion. 'You're in for it now, laddy.' With that, he turned on his heel and was gone.

Half an hour later, someone knocked on the office door. I opened it with trepidation.

'Trooper Humphreys?' barked a red-capped military policeman.

'Yep, that's me,' I replied with as much insouciance as I could muster, but knowing full well that I was in the deepest of deep shit.

'You're under arrest for insubordination and threatening a superior officer.'

Falling into line between the two military policemen, I was quick-marched to the guardroom. The adjutant came to inform me that I would be court-martialled for my disobedience and that he had been appointed to defend me. It seemed that my moment of insubordination had set me on what, for the military, was a well-oiled path, and

I could do nothing but accept its consequences.

My memories of the events that followed have faded into a blur as the years have passed. It is perhaps a good bit of self-preservation on my part; the fear and humiliation were so intense that I prefer not to remember. One thing I'll never forget is the line of officers, all in their dress uniforms, that had to be wheeled out on my account to hear my case. I was mortified and it really brought home the fact that I had breached two important principles of military law: always obey the last order, and never threaten a superior officer.

Eighty days' imprisonment in the army's notorious detention centre at Colchester in Essex was the verdict of the court. And so began the long journey – by ferry and then train – in handcuffs to the prison. It was a harsh place, with conditions much worse than anything I had experienced previously. We were always dressed in full battle order and everything was done at the double. The exercises were punishing and food was rationed, so I felt permanently racked with hunger. If I had thought the NCOs at the training camp were a bit over the top with their profanities and constant attempts to humiliate us, these guards managed to make an art form of it.

There was nothing for it but to knuckle down to the regime and hope that I wouldn't draw attention to myself. There was one interesting development. For the first time, I experienced drill with a rifle. In the cavalry we were only assigned pistols, as it was impractical to carry anything larger in the cramped confines of armoured vehicles. Learning to fire a pistol had been disappointing as I had never realized how wildly inaccurate the weapon was. It forever ruined my enjoyment of westerns, which until then had been considerable. Feats like hitting silver dollars tossed into the air were little more than fantasy, and down on the range, if I could place half the bullets assigned to me into a static life-sized target at thirty paces, I was entitled to consider myself a regular Wyatt Earp.

The rifle was a much more accurate and satisfying weapon, but unfortunately its primary function in the detention centre wasn't related to target practice. For breaches of good behaviour, the guards would order the offender to hold his rifle horizontally above his head with two hands and then run around the barrack square until told to stop. It was a gruelling punishment designed to break the spirit and I'm thankful I never had to endure it.

There's no denying that the regime at Colchester was much worse than that of a civilian prison. The military seemed to have been granted a licence to make its point – and I'm sure there would have been a public outcry if wardens in state prisons had been allowed to administer some of the punishments the military specialized in. Nevertheless, there were ways to reduce the severity of the regime, one of which was through religion. The padre, no doubt sensing that conditions were perfect for gaining new recruits to the Lord, always made himself personally available to any soldier who showed suitable contrition, and time had to be set aside for those who wanted to learn more from the scriptures. It was, for some, the perfect cop-out. I could tell the hard-nosed military police quietly fumed when an inmate declared an interest in the Lord's work, but as the padre would remind them, God had to come first. I'd had enough religious teaching at the Foundling Hospital and preferred to get on with the more physical exercises planned by the guards.

The army always seemed keen to convince us that we were doing God's work and should be proud to serve a higher power and purpose. As such, all ranks were obliged to participate in church parade on Sundays. But even with this religious grounding, suicide was an ever-present concern at Colchester. One of the guards' precautionary measures was to leave the light on all night in the billets and not allow any soldier to pull the bed covers over his head. This was hard for me at first, as I had always derived comfort from covering myself with my sheet all those years before. I had been able to forget about the others in the dormitory and enter my own little world, even if only for a few hours.

Somehow, my eighty days' detention, tough as it was, did not prove too onerous. Again my experience of life at the Foundling Hospital helped put the regime into perspective. If I could cope with harsh discipline and punishment as an infant, then I would not be broken when faced with it as a young man. I also had the consolation of knowing that I would be out by Christmas. This was not so for one particular lad in my billet. He became so depressed by the thought of spending Christmas inside that he decided on extraordinary measures.

At the centre of each billet was a heating stove with a concrete surround rising some twenty centimetres from the floor. Positioning his knee on the top of the surround with his foot sideways on the floor, he persuaded a friend to jump from the nearest bed on to the centre of his femur. A dull, stomach-churning crack announced the success of the enterprise: he would be invalided out.

My return to the regiment was a strange affair. Instead of the frosty reception I had expected for all the embarrassment I had brought the regiment, I was actually quite warmly received. It was as if nothing had happened. I can only assume my superiors knew of Colchester's grim reputation and had decided that I'd served my time. Obedience to orders was central to army life, and while this gave them no option, I don't suppose they took much pleasure in sending me – a young conscript – to such an unforgiving place. I later learned that the gleeful corporal had been hauled over the coals by the adjutant for provoking the incident.

Life in Northern Ireland was becoming dangerous again for the army. It was 1958 and the IRA had taken up arms once more, launching a guerrilla campaign against targets in Northern Ireland with the aim of throwing off British rule. There was an increasing air of seriousness about the base as we were aware that the IRA considered any soldier or policeman fair game. The Ulster Special Constabulary, a quasi-military police unit, was particularly loathed. Commonly known as B-Specials, these reserve policemen had been first deployed in the Irish War of Independence in the early 1920s. Almost exclusively Protestant and frequently drawn from criminal backgrounds, they were viewed with deep mistrust by Catholics. The army's role at this time was to support the civil power, which meant patrolling the borders alongside the Irish police and a number of B-Specials. This made me extremely nervous and I would always count down the hours until I could return safely to the base.

Ironically, though, it was within the grounds of the base that I found myself in trouble for the second time in my short military career. It was my turn to do guard duty at the camp armoury, which was built on the only high ground in the camp. Armed with a Sterling submachine gun, I paced back and forth round the block as the small hours of the morning ticked away. It was winter, and conditions were damp as well as cold. Some time shortly after three in the morning, I rounded an icy corner, lost my footing and crashed to the ground. My submachine gun followed, and as it did so, a shot rang out breaking the stillness of the night.

Picking myself up along with my weapon, I was gripped

by the awfulness of my predicament. Regimental standing orders dictated that if a shot were to be heard in the night, the only sensible assumption to be made was that the camp was under attack. Delaying to assess the situation would be to take a risk that could lead to disaster. The alarm was to be sounded and the entire regiment assembled on the barrack square. No time was to be wasted dressing. Only the soldier's helmet could be taken.

The image that flashed through my panicking head at that moment was of six hundred men in their pyjamas gathering to meet an attack that was not going to happen. Colchester beckoned all over again. I knew I had to act, and act fast. Rushing down the mound to the guardroom, I was astonished to find the guard commander slumped behind his small sliding window fast asleep. The realization then dawned on me that if the guard commander – the closest person to the gunshot – had not heard, then perhaps no one else had either. Furiously weighing my options, I decided to beat a careful retreat. I turned on my heels and with measured, slow steps and bending low – as if that would have made any difference – I began to tiptoe back up to the armoury. Suddenly, the silence was broken by a loud roar. I jolted upright and froze in my tracks.

'Oi! What the 'ell's going on? What are you doing there?' the guard commander bellowed.

I knew at once that the game was up and with a deep sigh turned to face him.

The following morning I was up before the adjutant on a charge of negligently performing my duty and abandoning my post. It was not to be Colchester, but instead 'jankers' – the quaint army term meaning 'confined to barracks' – for two weeks. Punishment duties were thrown in for good measure. It could have been worse, but I still felt mightily annoyed about the whole thing. Later, as I was contemplating my rotten luck, I realized that I couldn't have done anything differently. It wasn't my fault the path was slippery, and even if the commander hadn't heard, I wouldn't have been able to get away with the shot. This was because when the time came for me to be relieved, the bullets I had been issued with would have been counted and they would have seen that one was missing.

A worse fate lay in store for another soldier at the same armoury not long afterwards. The trooper at the centre of the incident had reached the end of his guard duty and was pulling back the bolt of his submachine gun to prove to his relieving office that it was empty of ammunition. But he failed to pull the bolt back far enough for it to engage, so when he took his hand away, the bolt shot forward, firing a bullet straight into the unfortunate soldier who happened to be standing opposite him and was also waiting to be relieved. Thankfully he survived, and as a bonus was excused the rest of his National Service. The bullet had gone through his shoulder and caused him to lose the use of one of his fingers.

I fully expected that my second fall from grace would not be dismissed as lightly as the first, but once again I managed to return to the regiment without any negative repercussions. I slotted back into army life and for a short while became 'batman' to a second lieutenant called Webb, who I felt was rather pompous. A 'batman' is essentially a personal servant assigned to a commissioned officer, and it was a duty that irked me no end. I thought that it was highly inappropriate to use conscripted men for such purposes. While I was prepared, along with others, to give two years of my life to defend the far-flung outposts of the Empire, I baulked at the idea that I should be compelled to spend such precious time acting as a servant.

Then I hit on what I thought was a bright idea. All regiments at that time were desperately worried about the imminent end of National Service and their bleak prospects of making up the shortfall. I could use my initiative – the same initiative that had served me so well during basic training – and set myself up as the regimental photographer. By offering to photograph all aspects of regimental life – its exercises, social life, responsibilities to the civil power and so on – I could put my camera skills to good use for recruitment purposes. The idea was that the images, which could be posted up throughout the regiment's traditional recruiting area in the North of England, would glamorize army life and convince young men to enlist.

The officers – indeed the same group of officers who

not long before had felt compelled to consign me to military prison – jumped at the idea of releasing me from the day-to-day tedium of soldiering to pursue the scheme. They even found the funds to equip me with a full-blown darkroom, complete with enlarger, chemicals and everything else I could possibly need.

It was a marvellous idea, and for the remainder of my National Service, officers and men alike were happy to make themselves available to my ever-snapping camera. When the Queen's sister, Princess Margaret, came to present new colours to the Regiment, there was the formerly errant me, camera in hand, shepherding all and sundry into position to have their pictures taken. And best of all, I thought, was when I came up with the proposal to photograph the whole regiment for posterity. Pointing this way and that, I bossed them all into line so that I could do the business. I had anticipated many of the soldiers asking for enlargements so they could have a personal record of their military service to take away with them – and I made a killing. It was a welcome boost to my allowance as a National Serviceman, which was a mere sixth of my civilian pay.

When, finally, after two years (plus the eighty days spent in Colchester), my demob date arrived, my discharge papers spoke only in glowing terms of my life as a soldier. A magnanimous veil was drawn over the colourful aspects, and when the time came to leave, the adjutant himself walked me down to the main gate.

31

Tom

A Life-Changing Meeting

It was shortly before Christmas in 1959 that my National Service came to an end. I was due to return to London to take up my old press agency job, but I wasn't sure whether that was the right path for me. I had itchy feet, and I felt the lure of a new life ahead of me with all its hopes and uncertainties. But before I could think about a fresh start, there was one matter that remained unresolved, and that was my family. Since leaving the Hospital I had thought often about my mother, though not with the same intense longing that I had when I was a child, partly because the strain of holding down a job and earning enough to look after myself had taken all of my attention. And yet the thought that I did indeed have a mother – one who might actually want to meet me – had refused to go away.

My discharge took place midweek from the army base in the lovely little market town of Barnard Castle in County

Durham. I had carried the knowledge that my mother was raising a family in Scotland with me ever since my kindly headmaster had allowed me to eavesdrop outside his office eight years before. I was, as it happened, equidistant between Dingwall, where my mother had been reported as living, and London, where I no longer wanted to be. I took it as a sign. There would be no better time or opportunity to journey further north, and if I was successful I could set the seal on a new chapter in my life.

I knew it was an undertaking fraught with risk. I couldn't be sure that my mother would be pleased to see me. Her refusal to allow me to be adopted had caused me to think that she might have kept a candle burning, but I couldn't count on this being the case eight years later. I knew nothing of the presents and cards she had sent to the Hospital over the years, as these had been withheld from me, and I had no way of knowing whether she had mentioned me to her husband or her children. If she hadn't and I turned up out of the blue, it could destroy her marriage. Even if her husband was aware of my existence, I felt certain that he would not be pleased to see me. Assuming that I could find my mother, I was determined to approach her in a way that would not risk alerting him or destroying the life she had created for herself in my absence.

The journey to Dingwall took me further north than I had ever travelled. I passed the magnificent structures of Durham Cathedral and Hadrian's Wall, and then Edinburgh with its grand streets and spectacular castle, before passing through Perth – 'the gateway to the Highlands' – and into the wild Highlands themselves. It was a spectacular rail journey, but as I sat there looking out of the window, I couldn't quite take it all in. My thoughts lay elsewhere. What would my mother look like? Would she be short or tall, fat or thin, pretty or otherwise? What would she think of me? How, even, was I going to introduce myself? And how, most important of all, would I get her on her own? Indeed, with no address, I wondered if it would be possible to locate her in the first place. It seemed to me that I had no other option but to adopt the riskiest course of all: to ring round the various law firms in the town to see if they had a Duncan Mackenzie working for them.

After ringing two firms and saying that I was an old army buddy who wanted to surprise him, I was told, on my third enquiry, that while they had had a Duncan Mackenzie working with them, he had left a few years before to take up a position in Edinburgh. I felt crushed. It was one thing searching for a person in a community of eight thousand, but quite another in a city of half a million. However, hope returned as the secretary on the other end of the phone told me to hang on while she asked a colleague the name of the firm Duncan had joined. She was gone for only a moment before returning with it, and also with the news that his wife, Jean, had returned to her old job as a legal secretary for Ketchen & Stephens – also in Edinburgh. She even provided me with an address.

It was all too good to be true, and I was not in the least bit fazed that I had had to journey almost to the very top of Britain to gain this information.

Hastening south, I arrived in Edinburgh early on Saturday morning. The thought hit me that nothing could be done until Monday, which would make things awkward as I was due to return to my old job first thing on Monday morning, so I decided to make a telephone call on the off-chance that someone might be in the office. I might get lucky and pick up some useful information that I could follow up that weekend.

The dice in that final month of the dying decade of the fifties continued to roll for me. A female voice answered the phone and confirmed what I had been hoping.

'Yes, Jean Mackenzie does work here. She's in this morning as it happens. Do you want me to put you through?'

'Oh no, no . . . Don't do that . . .' I stammered. The news that she was so close had stunned and completely wrong-footed me. 'I . . . Um, I think it'll be best if I catch up with her when she finishes. I want to make it a surprise. Please don't say anything about me calling.'

It was a heart-stopping moment. A separation that had lasted my entire life was about to come to an end. All I had to do was walk the few hundred yards from Princes Street and there would be the woman who had occupied my thoughts for so long. How would she view me? Would she be pleased? What if she wasn't pleased? Would she be the Ingrid-Bergman-like figure of my imaginings? How would we both handle the first meeting? Would this be the only one . . . ?

The walk towards Ketchen & Stephens was not like any walk that I had ever made before. I didn't notice a thing about the people or buildings I passed, impressive though I'm sure they were. I was aware only of my racing heart and a stream of unanswered questions.

On the doorstep that led up from the street, I paused to steady my rattled nerves. What would I say? What would she say to me? I shuffled around in the street for a few minutes trying to compose myself. Then I took a deep breath and made for the entrance. Climbing the few steps, I entered the hallway. I noticed a curved staircase to the right which led to the upper levels. It was extremely quiet, unnervingly so.

Further round to the right I noticed a desk, behind which sat a smartly dressed woman looking down at some papers. Suddenly, aware of my presence, she looked up.

'Can I help?' she enquired in a pleasant Edinburgh brogue. Relief swept over me as I realized that this was not my mother; she was too young.

'Yes, I believe Jean Mackenzie is in this morning,' I answered.

'Is she expecting you?' the woman enquired.

'No,' I replied.

'Well then, who shall I say is calling?'

'Bet— Better not say,' I said, stammering again. I could feel myself breaking into a sweat. 'It's a surprise, you see.'

The woman must have realized that I was the person who had made the mysterious phone call a little earlier. She gave me a sweet little smile and looked as if she was about to say something but then thought better of it. Lifting the phone, she pressed one of the numbers on the switchboard.

'There's someone to see you, Jean.' A pause followed. 'He won't say,' she replied to the voice at the end other end.

'She'll be with you shortly,' said the young woman, turning towards me with a quizzical look. Again she smiled sweetly before returning to her papers.

My heart was racing wildly now and I was trying to draw deep breaths but somehow struggling to hold any air in my lungs. The young woman offered me a seat, which I declined, and I started to pace a little. It was better, I thought, than standing like a tailor's dummy.

I thought my mother must be on one of the upper levels and I desperately wanted to look up in that direction, but I found it impossible. I purposely kept my back to the staircase. Then I heard a door open, followed by the sound of carefully measured footsteps coming down. At a certain point, the footsteps came to a halt, as though the person was taking time to study what was below. Then they resumed at a slightly slower pace. The footsteps reached the bottom and stopped again. After a slight delay, they made in my direction. Only when I knew that she was standing directly behind me did I feel compelled to turn round.

'Can I help you?' a softly spoken voice enquired. I observed a slim woman in her middle forties, still pretty and of medium height. Her hair was red with just a few flecks of grey showing. She gazed at me intently. An awkward silence ensued.

'Do I know you?' she asked.

'No, not really,' was all I could think to say. Then she paused again.

'Should I know you?' she whispered. How was I meant to answer that?

'In another world perhaps,' was all I could think to say.

The woman smiled, taking my hands into her own and gently squeezed them. A single tear ran down her face as she led me out into the street, still holding my hands. There she kissed and hugged me and pulled me close in a long embrace.

EPILOGUE

I FELT NO ANGER TOWARDS MY MOTHER during that first heart-stopping meeting, or indeed at any time after that. When she told me that I had occupied her thoughts for twenty years, and because her pleasure at meeting me was so obvious, I had no reason to doubt her. It was wonderful to hear that she had always wanted me, and at that moment, for the first time in my life, I felt that I truly belonged to someone.

That weekend passed in a whirlwind. After dabbing her eyes with a lace handkerchief my mother explained that she had to return to work and asked whether I would meet her in an hour at the McVities tea room on Princes Street. I felt some trepidation as I watched her vanish through the office doorway and into the darkness beyond, and although she only took forty-five minutes, the wait seemed like an eternity. It was a busy Saturday lunchtime in the tea room and I positioned myself at a table by the door so my mother would see me as soon as she came in. I shouldn't have worried; it was her favourite place to have lunch and the serving ladies knew her by name. I couldn't believe it when she introduced me to them as her oldest son. There was no shame or embarrassment or even an attempt to explain why I had an English accent. We talked about everything: my years at the school, George and Bessie, the army and the life I would be returning to in London. She seemed to hang on my every word and kept taking my hand across the table, as if to prove that I was really there.

On Saturday afternoon she took me home, having telephoned her husband Duncan at the office to prepare him for my arrival. I was warmly received by him and by my half-siblings, Maida, Katherine and John. They had no idea they had a twenty-year-old brother and were very excited by the revelation. My mother then called my father, who she'd been in touch with after a discreet and careful start so as not to upset either his or her spouse, and arranged to take me over to Glasgow to meet him the following day. She also rang her younger sister, Helen, and her brother, Jimmy – the baby of the family – and invited them to join us for a cup of coffee at a hotel in the morning so that I could meet everyone before returning to London.

I was nervous, knowing that a good first impression was key to being accepted into the family group. Helen and her lawyer husband, Bobby, were already waiting when we arrived. They had both known about me for years and said how pleased they were to be able to get to know me finally, but my mother's little brother, Jimmy, and his wife, Sheena, were quieter. I was impressed to learn that Jimmy worked for Rolls-Royce and tried to talk to him about the engineering and design process but he held back a little and seemed a bit hesitant to engage fully. I later found out that he had only been fifteen when Jean fell pregnant and had been kept in the dark about my birth for twenty years. He had always been close to my mother, and even though he was there to welcome me into the fold, it took him a little while to forgive her for keeping such a big secret from him. Both he and Sheena were very kind to me in the years following, and I recently travelled the eight-hundred-mile round trip to attend Sheena's ninetieth birthday celebrations. She is the last surviving member of my mother's generation and it is wonderful that she is still going strong and enjoying life in her own home.

Despite a little tension, that first family get-together was a happy one, with nervous smiles soon giving way to laughter as everyone relaxed and began to share their stories. There was one very important person missing from the celebration however – my maternal grandmother, Mary. And she would have celebrated. My mother became quite emotional when she told me that my grandmother, known to her family as 'Tan', had passed away six weeks earlier, and described how she had followed my progress at the

Hospital, sent me birthday and Christmas gifts every year – if only I'd known! – and given the Hospital two thousand pounds to be presented to me on my twenty-first birthday. This was the sum that the Hospital had provided so that I could buy photographic equipment after I was caught stealing from my ex-employer. It was astonishing. I wasn't told then that money was a gift from my grandmother, and I was bitterly upset to find this out too late to thank her. I learned that she had considered the loss of her first grandchild 'unfinished business', and that at the end it was my fate that troubled her conscience. She wished she had stood her ground all those years ago. It was distressing for me to discover that she had been prepared to face the consequences of her daughter's pregnancy, including the damage that a cruel, judgemental society would have forced on her family's life and standing, but had allowed her husband to prevail. As an elder in the local Kirk, he had been adamant. For my own part, I deeply regretted the ill-judged outburst that had consigned me to army deten-tion for eighty days. I never mentioned it to my mother, but if those days hadn't been added to my two years' National Service, I would have been discharged in time to meet my grandmother and bring her the resolution she so clearly craved. It might even have eased her passing.

After that enjoyable morning with my aunt and uncle, my mum and I caught the train to Glasgow so I could meet my father before heading back to London. Not wanting to intrude into the home my father had established with his wife, Audrey, she decided to wait for me in a nearby cafe.

Audrey knew about my birth and showed considerable kindness in welcoming me into her home. While my father stood by awkwardly, she motioned for me to take the armchair by the fire and headed into the kitchen to make some tea. There was an uncomfortable silence before he asked me about my journey from Edinburgh and how long I would be staying in the north. The tension was palpable and it was a relief when Audrey reappeared with a pot of tea and a plate of homemade shortbread. I took a piece, grateful for something to occupy my hands, but I found my mouth was so dry I could barely swallow the crumbs. Audrey helped to break the ice by saying that I was the very image of Raymond when he was a young man, and that meeting me was like stepping back in time. I found out later that my father's sisters – who had never liked my mother – had suggested to him that I was Hugo's child and this had caused him some unease. Audrey's remarks must have helped to allay such fears, and indeed the resemblance was uncanny; we were certainly cut from the same cloth.

My father represented something of a godlike figure to me, having been so recently a major while I was a humble National Serviceman. In fact I was awestruck when my mother told me his rank on the train, and I secretly wished

I could have shared this with my army buddies; they would have been mightily impressed. Perhaps the officers could have found a way to avoid sending me to Colchester if they'd known. I wanted to establish a rapport but that first meeting was a bit tense; there were long pauses in the conversation when neither he nor I knew what to say, and he seemed to have difficulty meeting my eye. Even though my father had known about me for a few years, he hadn't held me as a baby or pictured me as a part of his life and it would take time for our relationship to develop. We parted friends and promised to write, which seemed like a good way to start the process of getting to know each other.

There was so much goodwill during that first weekend with my mother that it wasn't long before I received an invitation to go and live with her and Duncan permanently. I wasn't enjoying my job with Paul Popper or the loneliness of life in the capital, and I leapt at the offer, seeing it as a chance finally to experience family life – with my own family. My mother proudly introduced me to all her friends, and Maida, Jean's nineteen-year-old daughter from her first marriage to Hugo, delighted in taking me under her wing – she was less than two years younger than me, after all. She made me go to Scottish country dancing lessons and set me up on dates with her friends; I was hopelessly awkward at both dating and dancing but at least my dating improved with time.

It was a happy day when Duncan brought up the subject of adoption. He used his role as a lawyer to condense the process, which usually took six months, into three so that the paperwork could be signed before I reached the age limit of twenty-one. Absurdly, my mother also had to adopt me as she had given up her parental rights when she had handed me over to the Foundling Hospital. I was truly pleased to become Tom H. Mackenzie, taking my family name and relegating Humphreys to an initial. I could have dispensed with it altogether, but this didn't seem right given that it had been an important part of my identity for a very long time.

When I returned to London nine months later in 1960, I kept in touch through letters and visits, and when I married my first wife Carole in December 1964, my entire family came all the way to London to wish us well. It was wonderful to see so many people who belonged to me gathered in one place, and their travelling so far only a week before Christmas seemed to set the seal on my future happiness. Even Bessie and Aunt May came to celebrate, though sadly without George, who had passed away some years before. I'd made amends with the couple shortly after meeting my mother by visiting them and apologizing for my wayward behaviour as an adolescent. It was a weight off my mind, and although I would never feel as close to them as I had done as a child, I enjoyed going over for supper and staying for the weekend occasionally. After

George died, Bessie seemed extra glad to have me back in her life and I was sorry to see less of her when I moved back up to Scotland to work in 1965, but we still managed to keep in touch, via my mother, rather strangely. She would travel down from Scotland to visit my sister Maida, who was living in Stoke Poges with her architect husband Alastair, and together they would make a point of driving over to see Bessie to take her out for the day. It was an odd relationship for me to fathom at the time, but on reflection I can see that my mother felt that it was the right thing to do: a way of saying thank you to the woman who had looked after her son for so many years when she could not.

Among the tragedies my mother suffered in her life was the loss of Duncan when he was killed in a road traffic accident in January 1965. I travelled to Edinburgh at once to be by her side and took this as a prompt to move back to the north permanently a few months later. I was working for a chain of health clubs at the time and managed to secure a transfer to manage the Glasgow branch. Supporting my mother through her grief strengthened our bond, and despite all those lost years, I have never felt anything but her son.

My relationship with my father took longer to develop. In fact, we never achieved the same closeness that I enjoyed with my mother. He used to write me long newsy letters and would buy the odd present too. I think he found the process of putting pen to paper easier than trying to work out what to say to me in the flesh. Sometimes, when we were with company, he used to pass me off as an old friend from his army days. Whether this was because he was embarrassed to have had a child out of wedlock or still had difficulty in thinking of me as his son, I'm not sure, but it saddened me. Perhaps the fact he had such a troubled relationship with his own father made it difficult for him to know how to respond to me in a caring and paternal way. I don't have many regrets, but I do sometimes feel that if I'd tried that little bit harder with my father, he might have been able to throw off the inhibitions of his Catholic upbringing and demonstrate the same level of affection towards me as he did towards his two daughters, Sally and Miriam, both of whom I have been close to since I first met them as children.

When it came to his sisters Audrey and Miriam, I had expected a frosty reception given all the trouble before I was born, but when I went to visit them, they both made an effort to be pleasant. Uncle Stanley, my father's older brother, was particularly kind and often invited me round to dinner. He had got into trouble with his parents for marrying a lovely woman called Grace who had driven buses during the war, and who they thought was too common, but she had the warmest heart you could imagine. She used to cook these absolutely huge meals, the biggest I've ever known; she and Stanley were very generous people.

The last piece of the jigsaw fell into place when, after more than thirty years, I managed to get in touch with my first foster mother, Elsie. I went to visit her and Monica, and it was such a happy reunion, we were all teary-eyed. I stayed the night in the old cottage at Alpha place, where Elsie still lived, and I even slept in my old bed. It was all a little bit surreal. The beautiful field we used to play in at the back was gone, swallowed up by a housing development, and I was deeply sad to learn that little Janet had passed away. She had a heart defect and had been warned not to have children, but craving a family of her own, she had ignored the advice. She died giving birth to her third child, and it had broken Elsie's heart; she had loved Janet as her own. We stayed in contact in the years following and Elsie even came to stay with me for a holiday in Plymouth.

In the late 1970s, my father and Audrey decided to get a divorce. The marriage had been a tempestuous one and I know they had both been miserable for a long time. After the break, Audrey continued to send me birthday and Christmas cards as well as photos throughout her life, and in this respect, as in so many others, I was lucky. Both my step-parents were good to me.

It seemed the perfect antidote to all the heartache when, after a gap of forty years, my parents rekindled their romance. It seemed to validate my own existence. It made me feel that I was not among those belonging to that loosely used and euphemistic term 'lovechild'; I was, beyond a shadow of a doubt, a real one – a real child born out of real love. Although they never married or lived together properly, my mother would go to stay with Raymond for long periods of time, and they were planning a holiday to South Africa to visit my half-sister, Sally, in 1990 when my father learned that he had cancer, and only a short time to live. So they never did make the journey they had been dreaming about in those months leading up to the outbreak of the Second World War. My mother nursed my father throughout his final illness and then returned to Glasgow after his death. She would often read the poems they had written to each other in their youth, and in her final years, she would even take out a photograph of him and quietly talk to him about her day.

My mother's end, when it came in 1998, was a peaceful one. She had a good death; suffering only the usual infirmities of old age, she simply sat in a comfy chair and passed away. Though five years older than my father, she outlived him by eight.

I was touched by how many people attended her funeral. As the eldest of her four children I stood at the front in line with my three siblings and shook each person's hand as they filed past, thanking them for remembering her. I realized as I stood there that I had taken over from her as the head of the family. It moved me deeply to have finally arrived at that status, having been brought up on the premise that we foundlings had none. For so many years my siblings had not even known of my existence, but now I was finally one of them – the acknowledged head of the clan, so to speak, with a suitable name to go with it.

As for my years in the Foundling Hospital, I harbour no bitterness, only thankfulness that it was there for me when I needed it, and I will always be grateful to the kind-hearted people who provided the means for the charity to do its work. Though the regime was a hard one, the people who administered it had faith in what they were doing to the extent that they believed they were doing God's work. And they did it well. They were true professionals. It is easy now, with the benefit of hindsight, to see where they went wrong, but we should remember that people thought differently then; they didn't understand the workings of a child's mind and how damaged a child might be never to know the warmth and love of family life. As Britain's oldest children's charity, the Foundling Hospital – now the Coram Foundation – is still, almost three hundred years later, a shining example of how a charity for underprivileged children should be run.

Despite their unpromising start in life, many of my fellow foundlings went on to make successful lives for themselves, becoming good mothers and fathers and valuable employees. Their success rate was vastly better than those presently passing through the care system, which is a sign that the Foundling Hospital got something right.

Perhaps its long tradition, stretching back over two hundred years, created an over-arching sense of family, much like the regimental system in the army. It certainly raised children to be tough and resilient, and its strong Christian ethos gave them a moral anchor.

We foundlings are now few in number – none are under seventy – but we remain a family to each other. We meet on a regular basis and have our own club, the Old Coram Association. Forged in the fierce fires of adversity and loss, we feel a particularly strong bond with each other, especially when we meet and reminisce. The touching suggestion has recently been adopted by the board of governors that when each of the three hundred or so surviving foundlings dies, a wreath will be placed in the museum in remembrance of them. They do not need to say sorry, but knowing what we know today of the needs of children and what suffering and loss can do to them, perhaps that is the unspoken message.

I know that I could not have achieved everything I have without the help and support of the Foundling Hospital. My life since meeting my mother has been a helter-skelter, roller-coaster ride. I have known desperate times as well as long periods of great success in business and in my private life as well. I have been married four times; two ended in divorce, and one happy union was sadly cut short by bereavement, but in the end the fates were kind to me. My health has remained remarkably robust; my businesses have prospered, and, at a time when I least expected it, I found love again; my domestic life has entered the happiest phase it has ever known.

I have fathered four children, although I lost one in infancy. My two strapping six-foot-plus sons are both high-flyers with their own businesses, and my daughter is trained in accountancy and specializes in taxation. All are in happy relationships. They have given me four grandchildren and I am proud of them all.

Pleasing too is the fact that I have morphed, at the grand old age of seventy-four, into a writer – not just of this book, but as a regular columnist for the *Plymouth Herald*. I was even nominated as their columnist of the year in 2013. It means a great deal to me that I am able to share my thoughts on life and what is happening in the world about us with the readers of my local daily paper. How proud tiny Miss Pickles, head of my infants' class, would have been of little Tommy. Instead of entertaining fifteen of her infants with his made-up stories during her absences from the classroom, he ended up entertaining a city.

ACKNOWLEDGEMENTS

My grateful thanks to my wife, Ausra, whose encouragement acted as a spur, and to my family members for their support, most of all to Grant, whose efforts throughout were unstinting.

My thanks also to Ingrid Connell, Jennifer Kerslake and Laura Carr for their sterling advice, and to the brilliance of the art department.

ACKNOWLEDGEMENTS

PICTURE ACKNOWLEDGEMENTS

All photographs from the author's own collection apart from:

Page 3, *middle*: Portrait of Captain Coram (*c.*1668–1751) 1740, Hogarth, William (1697–1764) / © Coram in the care of the Foundling Museum, London / The Bridgeman Art Library
bottom: A View of the Foundling Hospital, 1756 (engraving), Cole, Benjamin (1697–1783) / Private Collection / The Bridgeman Art Library

Page 4, *top*: The Foundling Hospital, Berkhamsted © Mary Evans / Peter Higginbotham Collection
middle: Boys in the Foundling Hospital, 3 May 1941 © Felix Man / Hulton Archive / Getty Images
bottom: Girls and boys in the chapel of the Foundling Hospital, 3 May 1941 © Felix Man / Hulton Archive / Getty Images

Page 8, *bottom*: Family portrait © Nic Randall

extracts reading groups
books competitions books new
discounts extracts
competitions
books new extracts discounts
events books extracts events
reading groups
events books
new extracts reading groups
new titles reading groups
interviews
reading groups events extracts extracts events
discounts books
new books events
events new events
discounts extracts discounts
www.panmacmillan.com
extracts events reading groups
competitions books extracts new